Cambridge Elements ≡

Elements in Ethics
edited by
Ben Eggleston
University of Kansas
Dale E. Miller
Old Dominion University, Virginia

MORAL PSYCHOLOGY

Christian B. Miller
Wake Forest University

CAMBRIDGE
UNIVERSITY PRESS

CAMBRIDGE
UNIVERSITY PRESS

University Printing House, Cambridge CB2 8BS, United Kingdom

One Liberty Plaza, 20th Floor, New York, NY 10006, USA

477 Williamstown Road, Port Melbourne, VIC 3207, Australia

314–321, 3rd Floor, Plot 3, Splendor Forum, Jasola District Centre, New Delhi – 110025, India

79 Anson Road, #06–04/06, Singapore 079906

Cambridge University Press is part of the University of Cambridge.

It furthers the University's mission by disseminating knowledge in the pursuit of education, learning, and research at the highest international levels of excellence.

www.cambridge.org
Information on this title: www.cambridge.org/9781108706438
DOI: 10.1017/9781108581011

© Christian B. Miller 2021

First published 2021

A catalogue record for this publication is available from the British Library.

ISBN 978-1-108-70643-8 Paperback
ISSN 2516-4031 (online)
ISSN 2516-4023 (print)

Moral Psychology

Elements in Ethics

DOI: 10.1017/9781108581011
First published online: May 2021

Christian B. Miller
Wake Forest University

Author for correspondence: Christian B. Miller, millerc@wfu.edu

Abstract: This Element provides an overview of some of the central issues in contemporary moral psychology. It explores what moral psychology is, whether we are always motivated by self-interest, what good character looks like and whether anyone has it, whether moral judgments always motivate us to act, whether what motivates action is always a desire of some kind, and what the role is of reasoning and deliberation in moral judgment and action. This Element is aimed at a general audience, including undergraduate students without an extensive background in philosophy.

Keywords: moral psychology, egoism, altruism, character, virtue, motivation, moral judgment

ISBNs: 9781108706438 (PB), 9781108581011 (OC)
ISSNs: 2516-4031 (online), 2516-4023 (print)

Contents

Preface

Within philosophy, the field of moral psychology has exploded in recent decades. In this short Element, there is no way to cover all of these developments. Instead, we will focus very selectively on the following big questions:

> Are we ultimately motivated by our own self-interest in everything that we do? Is there any evidence for genuinely altruistic or selfless, as opposed to egoistic, motivation? [Section 2]
>
> What is involved in being a good person, in having good character, and in meeting the standards of virtue? What are the virtues and vices, and are they possessed by most of us? [Section 3]
>
> What motivates us to act? Is it always our desires, or could a belief, or even something else, motivate us instead? [Section 4]
>
> When we judge something to be the right thing to do, are we always motivated to act accordingly? Or is it possible to be indifferent to what we genuinely think we ought to do? [Section 5]
>
> When we act on our moral judgments, are we typically acting on the basis of moral principles and moral reasons? Or is our behavior largely driven by nonrational intuitions or gut reactions, followed by a made-up story that we tell ourselves afterwards about the moral principles and reasons which supposedly guided our thinking? [Section 6]

To be sure, these are not the only big questions in moral psychology, but they are among the central questions that have dominated the field in the past fifty years.

Two omissions are worth noting. First, we will not look at moral epistemology, including the justification of moral beliefs and the implications of moral disagreement, since these issues are covered by Tristram McPherson in another Element.[1] Second, we will not delve into the literature on moral responsibility, since that is also covered in another Element currently in progress.

Intended Audience and Background

Moral Psychology is intended for a broad audience. I have tried to make it suitable for undergraduate students with some background in philosophy, as well as intellectually curious readers more generally. At the same time, I hope it will be of interest to academics whose work intersects with topics in moral psychology.

Unlike a scholarly monograph, this volume mostly focuses on offering an overview of several central debates in moral psychology. The goal is to provide a nonspecialist with a good lay of the land that can serve as a starting point for diving into some of the more advanced material in this field.

---

[1] McPherson 2020.

While much of the Element is an overview of the various topics, each section will end with my own view on the debate. I have written on various topics in moral psychology over the past fifteen years. One of the things that excited me about this project was the chance to go back to my own work – which is scattered across journal articles, edited volume chapters, handbook overviews, encyclopedia entries, and book reviews – and try to incorporate it into a coherent picture (I hope!) about how our minds work when it comes to moral matters.

1 Introduction to Moral Psychology

What is the field of moral psychology? There are many different ways of characterizing it, and I do not want to claim that any one way has to be adopted. Personally, I prefer to think of moral psychology broadly as the field of study in moral philosophy which is centrally concerned with better understanding what is involved in moral thinking, and how that thinking does and does not give rise to morally relevant action.

There is a lot packed into this. Let me first expand a bit on the 'moral' aspect, and then on 'moral thinking.' Finally, I will say more about how the field of moral psychology relates to moral philosophy.

1.1 The Moral

Let's start at a general level with the distinction between the normative and the descriptive.[2] Here are some *descriptive* statements:

"2+2=4"
"A water molecule is composed of two hydrogen atoms and one oxygen atom."
"George Washington was the first president of the United States of America."
"Benjamin Franklin was the first president of the United States of America."

These statements, as descriptive, only aim to capture the way the world actually is. Not all of them succeed in doing so, such as the fourth one about Benjamin Franklin. For descriptive statements, the key concern is whether the world is as each statement says it is.

Normative statements, on the other hand, are concerned with evaluating the way the world is:

"There should be more charitable organizations."
"He is a cowardly person."
"The criminal deserves the death penalty."
"If only he had acted for better reasons."

---

[2] Section 1.1 draws on Miller 2011, with permission of Bloomsbury Publishers.

Sometimes the descriptive and the normative come together. The statement that a person is cowardly may at once describe the person's actual character *and* also evaluate him as a person. But we know that the descriptive and normative domains often come apart. For descriptively the world as it *is*, falls short in all kinds of ways from the way that it *should be* normatively. There is war, but there should be peace. There is murder, but there should not be any murder. Examples abound.

Let's focus on the normative domain a bit more. Moral statements are a central part of the normative domain. But they are not the only part, as we can see below:

Prudential (long-term self-interest):
"Smoking is bad for you."
"Exercise will be good for you in the long run."

Aesthetic:
"That painting is beautiful."
"The room is tastefully designed."

Legal:
"This law is unjust."
"He should be sent to jail for breaking the law."

Religious:
"Communion should be served every Sunday."
"It is better for adults to be baptized rather than children."

Furthermore, these different normative domains can come into conflict with each other. For instance, it might be *legally* permitted in some societies to own slaves, but still be *morally* wrong to do so. Hence, in addition to each of these specific normative domains, there is also the idea of what we should do or what would be good to do, *all things considered*.

Unfortunately, philosophers have had little success in trying to clarify what makes a normative statement a specifically *moral* one. I do not have anything better to offer myself, and so in what follows I will simply adopt the attitude that we know a moral statement when we see it.

1.2 Moral Thinking

A number of different elements in our minds play an important role in our moral thinking. Here I will highlight three of them: beliefs, desires, and judgments.

We all have a host of *moral beliefs*. I might believe, for instance, that my friend is trustworthy, world peace is good, and this politician is corrupt. These count as *moral* beliefs because moral concepts are part of the contents of the beliefs (*trustworthy*, *good*, and *corrupt*). Of course, we have plenty of nonmoral beliefs too, such as my belief that 2+2=4, which can be very important as well to our moral thinking. My thoughts about whether someone told a lie or took a bribe or killed an attacker in self-defense involve nonmoral beliefs, but they can clearly factor heavily into my moral deliberation.

At the same time, I have plenty of moral *desires* too: desires with contents where moral concepts play a role. So I want to do the right thing, I want to become a better person, and I want my leaders to stop being so corrupt. Here too we have plenty of nonmoral desires, and again they can be very important to our moral thinking. An example is my desire to not say or do anything that would be embarrassing. Such a desire can influence my thinking so that I rationalize away why I didn't speak up in front of a group on an important issue.

A popular way to distinguish between beliefs and desires has been to appeal to differences in their *direction of fit*. Very roughly, the thought is that beliefs have a mind-to-world direction of fit – they aim to represent or capture the way the world is. If the belief is false, that is because it has failed to capture the world accurately. My belief that I teach at Wake Forest University aims to represent the way the world is, and fortunately it succeeds in so doing (since I really do teach at Wake Forest University!).

Desires, on the other hand, have a world-to-mind direction of fit. They aim to change the world (as seen by the desire) to have the world reflect the desire. Failing to capture the world is no fault of the desire. Rather, the fault is with the world in not reflecting what the desire aims for it to be like. If I want Wake Forest to win a national championship in college football (which I do), it is no fault of my desire if that does not ever happen (and, alas, it has not yet). I want the world to change so that Wake Forest has a national championship to its name, even if sadly it does not.[3]

Beliefs and desires, in turn, factor into the formation of moral *judgments*. Suppose I am deciding between three charities when trying to figure out where to make a donation to famine relief. I want famine to be eliminated. I also want to donate to the most efficient charity I can. On the basis of doing some research, I learn that one of the charities spends a lot of money on administrative costs. Another has a history of corruption. Eventually I form the moral judgment that I should make a donation to the third charity.

In this example, my moral judgment was formed through a process of moral deliberation, which is often understood as conscious and reflective. Sometimes,

---

[3] If we adopt a very broad understanding of 'desire,' then it could include wishes, wants, hopes, and intentions. Emotions such as fear and anger have been treated as belief-like or as desire-like by different philosophers, and we will not explore those debates here. For more on direction-of-fit accounts as well as their problems, see Sobel and Copp 2001.

though, moral judgments can be formed more immediately, such as when it is just obvious to me that, for instance, slavery is wrong. To the extent to which I reason to that conclusion, it would appear that the reasoning is happening under my conscious radar screen, subconsciously.

Finally, with respect to moral judgments, what should we say about them? Are they beliefs or desires? It turns out that this is a source of much controversy in the philosophical literature. The majority view, called *moral cognitivism*, holds that moral judgments are beliefs. But a minority view, called *moral noncognitivism*, holds that our moral judgments are, no surprise, desires. To make matters more complicated, there is some recent work exploring whether a hybrid account might be best, where moral judgments have both belief-like and desire-like dimensions. While not a focus of this Element, we will return to issues about cognitivism versus noncognitivism in Section 5.[4]

1.3 Situating the Field of Moral Psychology within Moral Philosophy

It is common to distinguish between three branches of contemporary moral philosophy: ethical theory, meta-ethics, and applied ethics.[5] How does moral psychology relate to them? First, a brief word of explanation about each.

Ethical Theory. Let's start with the claim that slavery is wrong. There are many possibilities for what makes it the case that slavery is wrong, including the pain and suffering it causes, how it violates the dignity of persons, and how it is cruel and inhumane. The ethical theorist attempts to sort through these options in order to arrive at the most promising account of the feature(s) which makes slavery wrong. More generally, the ethical theorist attempts to develop an understanding of what the relationship is between moral properties (such as wrongness) and nonmoral properties (such as causing pain). For example, on one ethical theory wrongness might be understood as a matter of causing pain. On another ethical theory, it might be understood as a matter of going against the commands of God. Leading ethical theories include utilitarianism, Kantian ethics, virtue ethics, and divine command theory.[6]

Meta-Ethics. Meta-ethics can be understood as the nonmoral study of the metaphysics, epistemology, and semantics of the moral. Unlike ethical theory, meta-ethical approaches are developed by examining the practice of morality from a disengaged perspective and typically refrain from making moral

---

[4] For more on moral cognitivism and non-cognitivism, see van Roojen 2018.
[5] Section 1.3 draws on Miller 2011, with permission of Bloomsbury Publishers.
[6] For a helpful introduction to ethical theory, see Timmons 2012.

claims. In other words, meta-ethics raises and attempts to answer questions *about* morality. To use an analogy, a scientist arrives at first-order scientific conclusions, whereas a philosopher of science examines the practice of science as such, and does not make any scientific discoveries. So too is the meta-ethicist not concerned, in the first instance, with arriving at new ethical claims, but rather with the answers to various questions about morality, such as the following:

> Do moral facts exist?
> If so, are they objective?
> If they are not objective, who or what created them?
> How do we learn the content of morality, if there is such content to
>   learn in the first place?
> What is the meaning of moral terms?
> Are moral statements capable of being true or false?
> If so, are any of them true?

A central goal of the leading meta-ethical positions is to answer questions such as these.[7]

Applied Ethics. As its name suggests, applied ethics examines the moral status of specific human actions and practices, including those which have become prominent in societal debates such as abortion, the death penalty, cloning, stem cell research, animal consumption, access to scarce medical resources, and so forth.

Where does moral psychology fit into these three leading areas of moral philosophy? The answer is that it is not confined to any one of them, but rather is important to all three of them.

Hence, as we will see in Sections 4 and 5, debates about motivation have been highly influential in meta-ethics, for instance. In normative ethics, Kantian, utilitarian, virtue ethical, and other approaches have had much to say about what our moral psychology should look like. And in applied ethics, one example where moral psychology is important is in trying to figure out how best to motivate people to change their behavior when it comes to, say, donating to famine relief agencies. These are just a couple out of a myriad of examples which highlight the importance of moral psychology to the different branches of moral philosophy.

Enough stage-setting, however. Let us dive into our first central issue in moral psychology.

---

[7] For a helpful introduction to meta-ethics, see Shafer-Landau 2003a.

2 Do We Ultimately Only Care About Ourselves? Egoism and the Alternatives

Let's begin with the following case, which we will return to in every section of this Element:

> *The Hospital Visit.* Sally breaks her leg in a skiing accident. She has been in the hospital for several days without any visitors, so she texts her friend, Franklin, tells him what happened, and mentions the name of the hospital in the hope that he will come to visit her.
>
> When Franklin reads Sally's text, he decides that he should go visit Sally in the hospital that afternoon. A few hours later, he walks into her hospital room. Sally is very glad to see him, and they have a very enjoyable time together.[8]

Franklin decided to visit his friend Sally in the hospital. That much we have already said. *Why* did he ultimately decide to go? This we do not know from the description of the case.

If the position in moral psychology called *psychological egoism* is correct, then we do know a bit more. The answer has to be that Franklin wants to benefit himself in some way. This is because, according to psychological egoism, everyone is ultimately motivated to benefit themselves in everything they do.

In the coming subsections, we will first unpack what the psychological egoist is claiming, and also see what some of the alternative positions are. Then we will look at three important philosophical objections which can be raised against the view. The section ends by shifting to the empirical literature, first with a brief summary of some results from dictator games, and then by reviewing a fascinating strand of research on empathy.

2.1 Clarifying the Positions

In Book II of Plato's *Republic*, one of the main characters, named Glaucon, recounts a famous myth about the Ring of Gyges:

> a shepherd ... saw there was a corpse inside that looked larger than human size. It had nothing on except a gold ring on its hand; he slipped it off and went out ... while he was sitting with the others, he chanced to turn the collet of the ring to himself, toward the inside of his hand; when he did this, he became invisible to those sitting by him, and they discussed him as though he were away ... he immediately contrived to be one of the messengers to the king. When he arrived, he committed adultery with the king's wife and, along with her, set upon the king and killed him. And so he took over the rule.[9]

---

[8] This case is inspired by an example from Stocker 1976. [9] Plato 359d–360b.

The main lesson of the story is not supposed to be about the shepherd. It is supposed to be about us. The claim is that if we had such a ring, we too would do whatever we thought would benefit ourselves. That might not take the same form as the shepherd's behavior, but nevertheless the focus would still be on ourselves.

Such a claim is an expression of psychological egoism. The view can be stated as follows:

(PE) The ultimate goal of each person's actions is the pursuit of his or her self-interest, subjectively understood.

What is self-interest? Loosely, we can understand it as what will benefit us in some way. Unfortunately, there are a myriad of theories trying to give a more precise definition. For instance, a *hedonistic* account of self-interest might describe benefits in terms of pleasure and the avoidance of pain. So, hedonistic psychological egoism could be written as:

(PE_{hed}) The ultimate goal of each person's actions is the pursuit of his or her pleasure and avoidance of pain, subjectively understood.

But a hedonistic account could be replaced with a variety of alternative accounts of self-interest, such as self-interest being what satisfies my desires or what promotes my flourishing. Fortunately for the purposes of this Element, we can remain at the generic level of just talking, as (PE) does, about self-interest.

Why the 'subjectively understood' in (PE)? Because it seems clear that we can be mistaken about what is in our self-interest. Someone might be motivated to experience pleasure from eating a fruit, for instance, only to bite into it and discover that it had gone bad and tastes rotten. For the psychological egoist, this action still fits the view since the goal is self-interest, from the person's own perspective.

Note that psychological egoism is both an empirical and a universal claim. It is empirical in that it attempts to describe how human beings actually are, rather than how they should be. It is universal in that it is making a claim about *all* human beings, without exception. Hence, strictly speaking, to refute psychological egoism one would need just one person performing one action for which (PE) is not true. At the same time, to really develop an interesting position in opposition to (PE), it would be better to claim something more substantive. For instance, one might try to argue that in certain conditions, *most* human beings are capable of acting in a way that does not ultimately involve the pursuit of their own self-interest. One possibility, to be explored later, is that sometimes we might be motivated selflessly by love for our closest family members.

Finally, psychological egoism is *not* the same thing as selfishness. A really selfish person never helps others in need. But it is quite possible for someone to be a psychological egoist and also deeply committed to charity work or volunteering for a good cause. Such a person would just be helping others as a means to pursuing his own self-interest as he sees it.

The opposite kind of motivation from egoistic motivation is *altruistic*. One version of psychological altruism claims that:

(PA) One ultimate goal for at least many people can be the pursuit of what would benefit another person, subjectively understood, regardless of whether the actor would benefit or not.

Less abstractly, if I am altruistically motivated, then I am ultimately concerned with what is good for another person. Whether I would benefit in the process is not my concern. For instance, when Franklin goes to the hospital to visit Sally, if he is concerned with just helping her during this difficult time, then that counts as being altruistically motivated.

Now, it is compatible with (PA) that one can be altruistically motivated and try to help someone else out while *also* benefiting from the action at the same time. So long as the benefit is merely a side effect or by-product, rather than the goal of the action, it would not detract from the action's being altruistic. To help with the distinction between a goal and a by-product, I like to the use the analogy of driving my car. My goal is to arrive at my destination, but a side effect (in this case a negative one) is that my car emits exhaust into the air. So too might it be the case that Franklin's goal is to just help Sally, and a by-product of the helping is that he also feels good about what he did.

Psychological altruism can be formulated in a variety of ways. As stated in (PA), it is a claim about *many* people. A very weak version of the view would be about just one person. A very strong version would be about all people. The very weak version might be true, but it is not very interesting. The very strong version is unlikely to be true. It is not clear that newborns are able to think in those terms. Also, psychopaths may be incapable of altruistic motivation, even if the rest of us are.

Of course if psychological egoism is true, then *none* of us is capable of altruistic motivation, or motivation whose ultimate goal is to benefit others. A stark way to bring out the contrast between the two views is as follows:

(PE*) For all human beings, altruistic motivation does not exist.
(PA*) For most human beings, altruistic motivation does exist.

Again, this is not the only way to develop the contrast between psychological egoism and altruism, but adopting this approach gives us a sharp juxtaposition between them.

It is worth stressing that the altruist is happy to grant that for much of the time, we are motivated by the pursuit of our own self-interest. Furthermore, she can and should grant that we often have more than one motive for our actions, so that cases of altruistic motivation can also be cases of egoistic motivation. Franklin might visit Sally both because he cares about her and wants to do what he can to help her for her own sake, *and* because he also does not want to feel bad as a result of not visiting her in the hospital.[10] The independent presence of the egoistic motive does not negate the existence of the altruistic motive.

Egoistic and altruistic motivation might seem like the only two kinds there could be. Not so fast. First, note that altruistic motivation is characterized in terms of *benefiting* another person. At least in principle, there could be motivation concerned with another person, rather than oneself, but not with benefiting that person – rather, it is focused on harming him, for instance. We will return to this in more detail in the next subsection.

More significantly, at least in theory there could be *dutiful* motivation, which is neither egoistic nor altruistic. If Franklin visits Sally because he thinks it is right and he is ultimately motivated to do the right thing, then that would count as dutiful.[11] Thanks to the work of Immanuel Kant in particular, dutiful motivation has been widely discussed in moral psychology. As we will explore in Section 3, Kant thought that it was the only kind of highly praiseworthy motivation there is.

Psychological altruists can be neutral about whether dutiful motivation exists. As far as their view is concerned, they do not have to take a stand. Psychological egoists, though, must reject dutiful motivation, along with altruistic motivation and any other kinds there might be, because they only accept motives which aim at benefiting oneself.

One final note of clarification about psychological egoism before we move on to assessing it. It is important to not confuse it with *ethical egoism*, which is the following view:

(EE) The ultimate goal of each person's actions should be the pursuit of his or her self-interest.

---

[10] "Feeling bad" can take a variety of different forms. For instance, a person could be motivated to do something to avoid feeling guilty, to avoid feeling ashamed, or to avoid feeling embarrassed. These would all count as egoistic motivations. Thanks to Dale Miller for noting the need to clarify this.

[11] Note that the "ultimately" is important here. If he is motivated to do the right thing, but that in turn stems from a deeper desire to make a good impression on other people, then his motivation would ultimately count as egoistic.

The key difference is that "should be" replaces "is." Recalling Section 1, ethical egoism is a view in ethical theory, and so is a competitor to views such as utilitarianism and virtue ethics.

Ethical egoism is specifying what makes actions right or wrong, and as such is neutral about the truth of psychological egoism. Thus, one could accept both that we should pursue our self-interest, and that we always do. Or, one could claim that we do not always pursue our self-interest, and that this is morally correct. Still another combination is to think that we sometimes are not motivated by self-interest, and in those cases we are doing something wrong. Finally, one might hold that we are always motivated by self-interest, but that this is a mistake.

For what it is worth, I join most philosophers in rejecting both ethical egoism and psychological egoism.[12] But we will only explore the latter in what follows.

2.2 Three Objections to Psychological Egoism

Here are three traditional philosophical challenges to psychological egoism that appeal not to data from empirical studies, but rather to our intuitions about particular cases. The empirical data will come in the next two subsections.

Extreme Heroism. Consider a case like the following:

> *Jumping on the Grenade.* Francisco is in a bunker with five of his fellow soldiers. He has grown close to all of them as they have fought together as a unit for many months. In the midst of a firefight, an enemy grenade is thrown into the bunker. No one besides Francisco notices the grenade. If it goes off, it will kill the other soldiers but he will not be harmed. Alternatively if he leaps onto the grenade, Francisco will die smothering it, but the other five soldiers will live. He leaps on the grenade and is killed immediately, but the others are saved.

There have been numerous such cases in wartime. This is not simply a philosopher's thought experiment.

On the face of it, cases of extreme heroism such as *Jumping on the Grenade* pose a challenge to psychological egoism. For it is hard to see what benefit one would gain by intentionally doing something which will result in one's death.

Admittedly, we can come up with egoistic explanations. Perhaps Francisco jumped on the grenade to receive rewards in the afterlife, or to gain fame after his death, or to avoid feeling guilty if he did not jump.

The critic of psychological egoism should grant that these explanations might apply in some cases. But two further points can still be made. First, is it plausible to think that jumping on the grenade was *always* done for one of these reasons,

---

[12] For problems with ethical egoism, see Rachels 1986.

and *never* out of concern, love, or caring for the soldier's friends for their own sake? Second, it is highly unlikely that any such egoistic calculating would have gone on in the soldier's mind, at least at the conscious, deliberative level. In the military, these decisions are often split-second ones, with no pausing to mull things over. As such, they could call into question the psychological plausibility of the egoist's story for cases such as *Jumping on the Grenade*.[13]

Extreme Hatred. Lex Luther might be so consumed with hatred for Superman that he is willing to do whatever it takes to make Superman suffer, even if it is at the expense of his own self-interest. Indeed, he is willing to be arrested, tortured, or even killed if that is what it takes to bring Superman down.

The thought here is that in cases of extreme hatred, a person's focus could be selfless in the sense that he is consumed with what harms another person, regardless of whether he benefits in the process or not. This would not be an altruistic desire, since it is not concerned with *benefiting* the other person. It is not an egoistic desire either, since it is not concerned with benefiting *oneself*.[14]

A natural reply to this kind of case is that Lex Luther could still be egoistically motivated because of the pleasure or satisfaction he would get from defeating Superman. But at this point the critic of psychological egoism can point to the distinction between a goal versus a by-product. Just because Lex Luther would be satisfied with defeating Superman, it does not mean that getting this feeling of satisfaction was his original goal. He wanted to see Superman go down in flames. This still would have been his goal even if he somehow knew ahead of time that he would not experience a feeling of satisfaction afterwards.

Love and Friendship. Consider the following argument about love:

(i) There are genuinely loving relationships.
(ii) If psychological egoism is true, then there are no genuinely loving relationships.
(iii) Therefore, psychological egoism is false.[15]

The relationships in question are not casual hookups or erotic flings. Rather, they involve the kind of love found in the best forms of parental love for a child, or in examples of two people who have been together for fifty years and are inseparable.

---

[13] A possible response at this point is to say that the psychological egoist is only giving an account of how we deliberate, and not of more reflexive behaviors that do not involve deliberation, as in at least many cases of jumping on a grenade. Thanks to Dale Miller for noting this response.

[14] For this kind of objection being used against psychological egoism, see Feinberg 1958.

[15] For related discussion, see Stocker 1976.

The key feature of this love is that it is other-oriented. The parent cares deeply about the good of her child for the child's own sake. She does not treat the child as a source of amusement or status for herself. That would be to instrumentalize the child, to make the child a mere means to her own benefit. If the parent were to do that, she would not love *her child*, but rather love something else which the child can provide.

The same can be said for spousal relationships. If it becomes clear that, say, a husband is only involved in the relationship because of what he gets out of it for himself – pleasure, comfort, status, security, or whatever – then his wife has good grounds for complaint that he does not really love her. Spouses who truly love each other can experience these other things too, but as side effects rather than as the primary goal.

Yet if psychological egoism is correct, then ultimately each person is motivated by the pursuit of his or her self-interest, and so is incapable of genuinely loving others. However, since there are cases of genuinely loving relationships, we should conclude that psychological egoism is not correct.

I will leave it up to the reader to decide how strong each of these objections is, and whether the psychological egoist can make a compelling reply. The remainder of this section looks to some empirical studies from behavioral economics and psychology which appear to have some bearing on the truth or falsity of psychological egoism.

2.3 Dictator Games

In the standard dictator setup, there are two people taking part in a study, one the 'dictator' and the other the 'recipient.'[16] To start, suppose $10 is given to the dictator, and she is told that she can give any amount between $0 and $10, inclusive, to another person. Whatever the dictator decides, that is the end of the story. So if the dictator wants to keep $8 and give $2 to the recipient, then that is what each person walks away with.

If we accept psychological egoism, as is standardly done in a traditional game-theoretic framework in economics, then we would predict that dictators will simply keep all the money for themselves. Since there is no threat of rejection by the recipient, and since all that matters is promoting one's self-interest, there is every reason to keep all of the money.

But that is not what most participants actually do. In a study by Robert Forsythe and his colleagues, while 21% gave nothing to the recipient, the remaining 79% gave something, with 21% giving an equal amount of the

---

[16] Section 2.3 is adapted from Miller 2015, with permission of the Stanford Encyclopedia of Philosophy.

$10.[17] Daniel Kahneman also ran a version of a dictator game where students in a psychology course could divide $20 evenly with an anonymous fellow student, or keep $18 for themselves and give $2 to the other student. Strikingly, 76% choose the even division.[18] In addition, 74% of participants were subsequently willing to pay $1 to punish an unfair dictator and in the process reward a fair one, even though this would reduce their own monetary payment.[19] Overall, according to one review of the literature, giving in dictator games amounts to roughly 15–20% of what a participant receives in the first place,[20] which is less than fair but more than completely self-interested.

So, it looks as if psychological egoism makes the wrong prediction by saying that dictators will keep all the money, and on these grounds the view can be called into question by this research. However, over time, more sophisticated studies were carried out which fit an egoistic story. Here is one such example:

> In the baseline condition of John List's study, both people in the dictator game setup were given $5 to start with. Then the dictator received another $5 and was given the chance to allocate anywhere from $0 to all $5 to the other person. Three additional conditions had interesting twists. In the Take ($1) condition, the setup was the same, including the chance to allocate money, but now instead there was an option to take $1 from the other person. The Take ($5) condition, as its name suggests, allowed up to $5 to be taken from the other person (or up to $5 allocated, or nothing taken or allocated). Finally, in the Earnings condition, everything is the same as Take ($5) except the dictator earned the $10 for performing a 30-minute task beforehand. Here were the results:[21]

	% Giving a Positive Amount	Average Amount Given[22]
Baseline	71%	$1.33
Take ($1)	35%	$0.33
Take ($5)	10%	−$2.48
Earnings	6%	−$1.00

Strikingly, when given the chance to take money from a stranger, dictators would less frequently allocate money to the stranger, and their average allocation would be smaller. We see this in the change from Baseline to Take ($1). The pattern continues to an even greater extent when more money is involved in Take ($5) as

---

[17] Forsythe et al. 1994: 362.   [18] Kahneman et al. 1986: S291.   [19] Ibid.
[20] Camerer 2003: 57–58.   [21] List 2007: 487.
[22] It is not clear from List's article whether these averages reflect just those cases where money was given or taken, or whether they include dictators who did nothing (such as the 29% in the baseline condition). Thanks to Ben Eggleston for noting this.

opposed to Take ($1). This all seems to fit with an egoistic picture of our psychology. Plus, if they felt like they earned the money as opposed to just being given it by the experimenter, then almost none of the dictators would be willing to part with their money, being more inclined to take rather than to give.

Several more sophisticated egoistic motives have been proposed to account for the behavior of dictators. Here are a few examples:

A desire to feel good by giving.

A desire to not appear selfish, or to appear to be fair.

A desire to give what others expect one to give (or not to give).[23]

Hence, it seems that we will have to look elsewhere if we are going to find studies that cause trouble for psychological egoism as expressed in (PE).

2.4 Batson's Empathy-Altruism Hypothesis

We can indeed find such studies in the form of the research that psychologist Daniel Batson from the University of Kansas has done over many decades.[24]

The key starting point for Batson is *empathy*. When I genuinely empathize with what another person is going through in a time of need, several steps are typically involved. I first try to understand what the person in need is feeling from her perspective, rather than mine. Then, because of this understanding of her feelings, I come to form similar feelings myself. Finally, these feelings I am now having can cause sympathy and motivation to act in some way to help the other person.

Hence, when he received Sally's text, Franklin might have tried to imagine how she was feeling, all alone in the hospital. He might have come to develop feelings of distress himself. And, finally, he might have been moved to go and visit her. If so, his action would have been driven by his empathetic feelings.

Now, by itself nothing about this characterization of empathy needs to be incompatible with psychological egoism as understood in (PE). Even if he visited Sally as a result of feeling empathy for her situation, he still could be going to, for instance, relieve the distress that has been caused within him. But what is striking about Batson's research is that he and his colleagues have found impressive support for what he calls the *empathy-altruism hypothesis*, or the claim that "empathy evokes motivation directed toward the ultimate goal of

---

[23] For an overview, see Dana et al. 2006: 194–195, 200, Dana et al. 2007: 68–69, 78.

[24] Section 2.4 is adapted from Miller 2013: chapter five, with permission of Oxford University Press.

reducing the needy person's suffering; the more empathy felt for a person in need, the more altruistic motivation to have that need reduced."[25] In other words, the claim is that empathy can lead to the formation of a desire which is both altruistic and not derivative from a deeper self-interested desire. It has as its object the good of the other person – namely, that her suffering, ailment, or distress be alleviated.[26]

Given how empathy is being understood, the empathy-altruism hypothesis should not be surprising. It does not involve the egoistic mindset of imagining how you would feel if *you* were put in the same situation as a person in distress. Rather, it requires stepping outside of your own perspective. You have to focus just on *what the other person* is going through, including what emotions and feelings she is wrestling with in the situation, and what those emotions and feelings are about. As Batson's instructions to his participants indicated, "try to imagine how the person being interviewed feels about what has happened and how it has affected his or her life."[27] This kind of focus on another's feelings of distress or sadness can touch a person, causing feelings within him which can motivate a search for ways to reduce or eliminate that other person's distress for its own sake.[28]

In order to test this hypothesis, Batson had to examine a number of competing egoistic explanations, and he cleverly devised experiments for testing each of them. In every case, no empirical support has been found for the egoistic explanations. Covering Batson's treatment of all these explanations is beyond what we can do here, but I will at least combine the egoistic explanations into three categories and see what a representative experiment looks like for testing each of them.[29]

(i) Aversive Arousal Reduction. According to this egoistic strategy, feeling empathy is thought to be unpleasant or distressful for the person experiencing it, which in turn generates motivation to end such feelings. One such means to do so is to help the person in need and so the observer is motivated to help, but only

---

[25] Batson 2002: 92.

[26] Note that there can be egoistic or other kinds of desires which *also* play a partial causal role in giving rise to the behavior.

[27] Batson et al. 1997: 753, emphasis removed.

[28] Again it is worth stressing that the claim is *not* that the person who empathizes is motivated to help in order to eliminate feelings of personal distress that have formed in him as a result of empathizing with the distress of another person. That would make the motivation to help ultimately egoistic. Rather the claim is that the person who empathizes is motivated to help at least in part in order to try to relieve the distress of the other person, *independently* of whether he would benefit in the process.

[29] The three categories used follow Batson 2002: 94. For reviews of the experimental support for the empathy-altruism hypothesis, see Batson 1991, 2002, 2011.

as a way of making himself feel better.[30] If this explanation is correct, then helpful actions done in this way would not be altruistic.

One way to experimentally test this proposal is to provide participants with an opportunity to escape being around the person in need. If they are primarily motivated by seeking ways of reducing their distress, then they will take the opportunity to escape without helping.

But this is not what happened in the experiments. For instance, in Toi and Batson's study, undergraduate participants were given more objective versus empathy-inducing instructions for listening to a (fictional) broadcast about a classmate's auto accident.[31] Some of the participants were told that their classmate would not be coming back to their psychology class. Others were given a more difficult to escape scenario in which they were told that she would be attending all the remaining classes and, given that she would be in a wheelchair, she would be hard to avoid. When given a chance to help her, here is how participants in the different groups responded:[32]

Ease of Escape	*Objective Instructions*	*Empathy-Inducing Instructions*
Easy	33%	71%
Difficult	76%	81%

Thus, participants feeling empathy for their classmate did not appear to be significantly motivated to find ways to reduce their feelings of distress, unlike participants who took a more detached perspective.[33]

(ii) Empathy-Specific Punishment. Another family of egoistic explanations maintains that people who feel empathy for those in need are motivated to help primarily in order to avoid one or more punishments for not helping. Such punishments can range from third-person disapproval, such as social or religious condemnation, to first-person disapproval, such as guilt or shame.[34] Thus, again, motivation would not be ultimately altruistic toward those in need in such

---

[30] For discussion, see Toi and Batson 1982, Batson 2002: 94–95, 2011: 111–114.

[31] The key differences in the wording of the instructions were, in the objective condition, "Try to be as objective as possible, carefully attending to all the information presented about the situation and about the person who is being interviewed. Try not to concern yourself with how the person being interviewed feels about what has happened"; versus in the empathy-inducing condition, "Try to take the perspective of the person who is being interviewed, imagining how he or she feels about what has happened and how it has affected his or her life. Try not to concern yourself with attending to all the information presented" (Toi and Batson 1982: 285).

[32] Ibid., 288.   [33] For additional studies, see Batson 2011: 111–114.

[34] For discussion, see Batson 2002: 95–96, 2011: 114–121.

cases, since those empathizing would be concerned mainly about themselves and what they can do to avoid the relevant form of punishment. Hence, psychological egoism would hold after all.

One way to test at least some explanations which fall under this category is to look at the change in mood of study participants when told that their attempt to help someone in need failed. If empathy-specific punishment is what is going on, there should be a noticeable difference in mood between participants who were told that their failure to help was justified and those who were told that it was unjustified. In particular, if participants are told that their failure was justified, we would expect them to be greatly relieved, whereas if it was unjustified, then they should be highly distressed. After all, if their failure was justified, there would be no grounds for legitimate punishment. However, if the empathy-altruism hypothesis is correct, there should be little to no mood change between justified versus unjustified failures as the person is concerned only with helping the other in need, and the need still has not been addressed.[35]

Batson and Weeks (1996) carried out a study with precisely this design. Participants were students at the University of Kansas who first took a survey assessing their current mood. They then learned about a (fictional) person in need, Julie, who would be receiving a series of mild but uncomfortable shocks if she did not perform well enough on a task given to her. Participants learned that they could help Julie by doing well on a task of their own (a number search), and if they performed well enough Julie would receive an extra minute of time for her work. Next, half the participants were given a set of objective instructions, and half were given a set of empathy-inducing instructions, before they listened to a recording of Julie express her anxiety about having to receive the shocks ("Well, they gave me a couple of sample shocks so that I'd know what to expect. Wow! [Nervous laughter]").[36] Then it was time for participants to actually do the number search, which was graded by the experimenter. Everyone was told they didn't do well enough to help Julie, but some were comforted with the information that the task was "Absolutely Impossible," whereas others were not let off the hook because it was "Moderately Easy" (70% of the other students did it just fine!). The participants then learned that Julie did not complete her own work in time (but maybe she would have with the extra minute), and so ended up receiving the shocks. Participants completed another mood survey so that the researchers could assess their change in mood from beginning to end. Using a nine-point mood scale, here is the average change in mood that was discovered after participants learned of their failure to help Julie:[37]

---

[35] See Batson and Weeks 1996: 148–149, and Batson 2002: 95–96.
[36] Batson and Weeks 1996: 150.   [37] Ibid., 152.

	Objective Instructions	Empathy-Inducing Instructions
Failure was Not Justified	−2.23	−3.17
Failure was Justified	−1.25	−2.83

The fact that there is no statistically significant variation between the numbers on the right-hand side strongly suggests that participants were concerned about preventing Julie's suffering, rather than about whether they would be punished for not helping her.[38]

(iii) Empathy-Specific Rewards. The third class of egoistic explanations for empathy-induced helping centers not on punishments but on rewards. It claims that people in such cases are ultimately motivated by one or more of the specific rewards attached to helping the person in need with whom they empathize. Such rewards might come in the form of social or religious benefits, or more internal feelings of joy, honor, pride, or pleasure.[39] Once again, these would not be altruistic motives for helping.

One way to test these reward explanations is to examine differences in mood based upon whether the problems of the person in need are relieved by the empathizer or by a third party. If empathy-specific rewards are the motivating force behind helping, then comparatively speaking there should be a much higher mood in those who address the need *themselves* than in those who observe the need relieved by someone else. According to the empathy-altruism hypothesis, on the other hand, it should not matter who is helping the person in need so long as that need is addressed.[40]

Experimental support for this kind of egoistic explanation has not been found. Batson and his colleagues (1988) devised a study in which participants were initially told that their performance of a helping task would influence the number of electric shocks someone else would receive. Similar to the previous study, they then heard a recording of the other person expressing concern about being shocked. Two types of experimental variables were introduced separately before any shocks could be delivered:

---

[38] For additional studies which challenge the empathy-specific punishment hypothesis, see Batson 2011: 114–121.

[39] For discussion, see Batson 2002: 96–97, 2011: 122–131.

[40] See Batson et al. 1988: 53, and Batson 2002: 96–97.

Some participants were notified that the other person has now been spared the shocks by being reassigned to do something else that does not involve shocks. The remaining participants were notified that the other person's situation remains the same.

Some participants were told that they no longer have an opportunity to help reduce the number of shocks the other person would receive. The remaining participants were told that they still have the opportunity to help reduce the number of shocks.

Hence, some participants would find themselves in the scenario where, by doing their helping task well, they could spare the other person from receiving shocks. But in one of the other scenarios, if the helping task is done but the other person has already been reassigned away from something that involves shocks, then there would be no suffering, but not because of anything the *participant* did to help. If the above egoistic explanation is correct, we would expect significant variations on the mood scores of the participants, based upon whether *they* were the ones whose helping made a difference or not.

Instead, Batson found that the average mood of participants at the end of the study, rated from 1 to 9 (with 9 being good), was as follows:[41]

	Participant Does Helping Task	**No Opportunity to Help**
Other Person Avoided Shock Task	6.29	6.73
Other Person Does not Avoid Shock Task	6.56	5.84

The key takeaway is that there was no significant difference found in the participants' mood "when the victim's need was relieved by their own action than when it was relieved by other means."[42]

Stepping back from these different egoistic accounts, the general point is this: according to more than thirty different experiments carried out by Batson and his colleagues, there is no evidence that high levels of empathy generate egoistic motivation to help. In fact, all the leading egoistic explanations seem to be empirically disconfirmed.

At the same time, this conclusion should be taken for what it is. While it is true that a number of particular egoistic hypotheses have been tested, new and

---

[41] Batson et al. 1988: 56. Batson also reports data on change in mood as well.   [42] Ibid.

more subtle ones continue to be proposed.[43] There is also the possibility that a hypothesis using multiple egoistic motives could be true.[44]

My own view is that the balance of the empirical research does not conclusively demonstrate that psychological egoism is false. However, it does seriously call it into question. When combined with the three objections that were raised in Section 2.2, I think we have good reason to accept that there are other kinds of motives besides just the egoistic ones.

As we will see in the next section, this is good news, since if psychological egoism were true, then good character would not exist.

3 Good Character: What Is It, and Does It Even Exist?

Franklin does what you might expect a person of good character to do. He goes to visit his friend Sally in the hospital when he finds out that she has broken her leg. But does he really have a good character? What does it take to have a good character? Do most people have a good character, a bad character, or something in between? These are the main questions we will take up in this section.

3.1 Good Character, Virtue, and Vice

A person can be described as 'good' in a variety of ways. She might be a good soccer player, or a good artist, or a good philosopher. Since our focus is on moral psychology, what is especially relevant is understanding what is involved in being a morally good person. Here it is common to assume the following:

> A morally good person is, among other things, someone who has the moral virtues.[45]

In contrast,

> A morally bad person is someone who has the moral vices.

This then turns our attention to unpacking what a moral virtue and a moral vice are. Let's start with the virtue of compassion, and return to Franklin's visit to see Sally.

We can agree that, in and of itself, Franklin's action is a compassionate act. But that does not entail that he is a compassionate *person*. Suppose we add to the story that he never helps out anyone else in need. Sally is the only exception.

---

[43] For additional egoistic hypotheses, see Stich et al. 2010. For responses, see Batson 2011: 120–121, 135–145.

[44] For related discussion, see Stich et al. 2010: 201, and Batson 2011: 132–134.

[45] The "among other things" could include following her conscience, being motivated to avoid wrong actions, and other commonly assumed features of a morally good person. Thanks to Dale Miller for noting this.

Even in her case, his helping is sporadic and unpredictable. I think we can then say that Franklin is not a compassionate person.

Now, let's change the story so that Franklin does reliably help others in a variety of different circumstances where there are opportunities to help (to use a fancy label, his helping is 'cross-situationally consistent'), and this pattern continues reliably over time (here the fancy label is 'temporally stable'). If we knew these facts about Franklin, would that be enough to conclude that he is a compassionate person?

Controversy arises at this point surrounding questions of motivation. Let's add to the case that, while Franklin's behavior is reliably helpful, he is acting this way solely to make a good impression on others. If it were not for the positive self-benefits, Franklin's helpful behavior would diminish significantly.

Does motivation matter to being a compassionate person, or more generally to being a virtuous person? More precisely, does it matter in and of itself, or 'intrinsically' as philosophers like to say, independently of whatever behavior it might give rise to? Some say that it does not, and that what really matter are just the good outcomes that are produced by the behavior. On such an approach, it is possible to be motivated by self-benefit and still be compassionate, so long as the egoistic motives contribute to the good outcomes.[46]

On the other hand, many philosophers working on virtue would maintain that motivation of the right kind – the intrinsically virtuous kind – is necessary for having a virtue, independently of whether that motivation contributes to good outcomes or not. So if Franklin is motivated to help only out of a desire to make a good impression, then while his helpful actions could be beneficial to others, they would not arise from the virtue of compassion.

This distinction between intrinsically virtuous motives and outcomes gives us three main options for understanding what a virtue is:

(V1) Something is a virtue for a human being only if it contributes to the person's reliably bringing about good effects in the world. The actions being caused by intrinsically virtuous motives is not necessary, although motivation is still important since it influences which actions and subsequent outcomes are brought about.

(V2) Something is a virtue for a human being only if:
   (i) it contributes to the person's reliably bringing about good effects in the world,
   and

---

[46] For an influential discussion of what is called a 'consequentialist' approach to the virtues, see Driver 2001.

(ii) it gives rise to virtuous actions which are produced by intrinsically virtuous motives.

(V3) Something is a virtue for a human being only if it gives rise to virtuous actions which are produced by intrinsically virtuous motives. Reliably bringing about good effects in the world is not necessary.[47]

For what it is worth, my own view is that we should accept the third option.

I am persuaded that motivation matters because of my intuitions about certain examples. For instance, it seems clear that if Franklin only helps others out of a desire to make a good impression, no matter how helpful the actions themselves might be, he does not thereby count as a compassionate person.

A second reason why motivation seems to matter is that virtue is praiseworthy. Yet while virtuous motivation is praiseworthy, sometimes good outcomes are not under our voluntary control. Rather, they are often dependent on luck.[48] For instance, consider this case:

> *The Unlucky Farmer.* Every weekend for many years a farmer donates his surplus vegetables to a food shelter and does so primarily because he cares about those who are less fortunate. But it turns out that the food is contaminated by a microscopic bug, which does not have any immediate health effects, but years after ingestion causes serious gastrointestinal complications. The farmer had no way of reasonably being aware that the bug was there. He followed every safety precaution that any farmer would be expected to follow, and for years no one ever reported getting sick from the vegetables.

In this case, it seems to me that the farmer could still be a compassionate person. We would need to know more about the cross-situational consistency and the stability of his helping in other kinds of circumstances besides this one, but there is nothing about this case that strikes me as incompatible with his being a compassionate person. In particular, the negative long-term outcomes do not detract from his being compassionate.[49] On the other hand, a different motive could have detracted. If instead he made the donations just for the tax write-off, then that undermines his acting from the virtue of compassion. These intuitive results align with (V3) better than its rivals.

---

[47] For more on these options, see Battaly 2015.

[48] For more on this argument, see Battaly 2015: 60.

[49] Note that the example says that he is *reliably producing* bad long-term outcomes, rather than just doing so in one particular instance. As Dale Miller reminded me, someone who thinks that a virtue must reliably produce good effects does not think that it must *always* or *invariably* do so. There can be particular instances where it does not. In *The Unlucky Farmer*, though, the farmer is disposed to act in ways that, as a matter of fact, repeatedly bring about bad outcomes in the long run.

What kind of motivation counts as virtuous? One approach is to try to answer this question for all the virtues at once. But this, I think, is too simplistic. To illustrate why, let's start with compassion, and make use of the division of motives from Section 2 into three categories:

> *Egoistic Motivation*: If the ultimate goal is to benefit myself, then I am not exhibiting compassion toward someone in need. Hence, Sally has every right to complain about Franklin's lack of compassion if he tells her that he is only visiting to help get rewards in the afterlife, or to not feel guilty if he does not visit.
>
> *Altruistic Motivation*: If the ultimate goal is to benefit the other person in need, then this can be an expression of compassion.
>
> *Dutiful Motivation*: If the ultimate goal is to do my duty or do the right thing, then I am not exhibiting compassion toward someone in need. Imagine how Sally might react if Franklin were to tell her that he only came to see her because he thought it was his duty to do so, or that he had a moral obligation to visit. She might be troubled by this response, finding it cold and impersonal. It leaves out the most important element, which is any special connection to her.[50]

So, from this breakdown, we can conclude that:

> The virtue of compassion requires altruistic motivation.

But now switch to another virtue, honesty, and let's see what happens:

> *Egoistic Motivation*: If the ultimate goal is to benefit myself, then I am not exhibiting honesty. If Florence does not cheat on the test when she has the opportunity to do so, that is an admirable action. But if her motive was simply fear of getting caught and punished, then the action did not stem from the virtue of honesty.
>
> *Altruistic Motivation*: If the ultimate goal is to benefit or at least not harm another person for his or her own sake, then this can be an expression of honesty. Such would be the case if instead Florence does not cheat on the test because she respects Professor Miller.
>
> *Dutiful Motivation*: If the ultimate goal is to do my duty or to do the right thing, then I can be exhibiting honesty. In this version, Florence responds when asked about why she did not cheat by saying things like "It would have been the wrong thing to do," "It goes against God's morality," or "It would not be honest." These can be compatible with Florence acting from the virtue of honesty, it seems to me.

Given this breakdown, we might conclude differently this time that:

> The virtue of honesty requires either altruistic or dutiful motivation.

---

[50] For an influential discussion of this point, see Stocker 1976.

More generally, the motivational profile of each virtue needs to be examined on a case-by-case basis.

This discussion can also invite the thought that:

No virtue reliably gives rise to egoistic motivation to act.

Admittedly, this is a controversial claim. And until we go virtue by virtue to test it, it is premature to jump to this conclusion. But it is a claim that I at least find appealing.

These observations about virtuous motivation connect up in important ways with the previous section. For if psychological egoism is true, then all of our actions are ultimately motivated by what we think is in our own self-interest. Altruistic motivation would not exist, since altruistic motivation aims at promoting the good of others independent of self-benefit. So if psychological egoism is true, and compassion requires altruistic motivation, it would follow that:

No one is a compassionate person.

Same with psychological egoism and honesty requiring either altruistic or dutiful motivation:

No one is an honest person.

Most striking of all, if psychological egoism is true, and no virtue reliably gives rise to egoistic motivation to act, then none of us has ever had any of the virtues. That is a bold (and distressing) thought.

Fortunately, we saw that there is good reason to doubt the truth of psychological egoism. For instance, if Batson's research holds up, then empathy is a source of altruistic motivation, and is indeed the only source that has been empirically supported in detail. So, given what we know now, it would follow that:

If someone is compassionate, then empathy is playing a central role in giving rise to her altruistic motivation.

Hopefully, empirical support for other sources of altruistic (and dutiful) motivation will emerge in future research.

3.2 Other Categories Besides the Virtues

Even if psychological egoism does not rule out our chance of becoming virtuous, still it is hard to think that we are all morally good people. So, what are the alternative categories we might use to better understand someone's character?

One obvious category is vice. Corresponding to honesty is the vice of dishonesty. For courage it is cowardice. For generosity it is stinginess. And so on.

It is natural to think of moral vices as structurally similar to moral virtues, but just oriented in a bad or evil direction. So, for instance, one does not count as dishonest by telling lies only in the courtroom or only on one day of the year. There has to be some cross-situational consistency and stability over time.

There is also a parallel controversy over whether vice requires appropriate vicious motivation or not, and, similarly, with whether it requires bringing about bad outcomes or not. To test intuitions, consider this example:

> *The Cruel-Minded Doctor.* A doctor has come to detest his patients, and has devised a plan to secretly kill them. He will introduce a slow developing but ultimately deadly disease into his patients' annual flu shot. When the time comes, he administers the shot. But the disease does not end up developing. Unbeknownst to the doctor, his patients had all been vaccinated against the disease when they were infants.

In this case, the doctor does not cause any harm to his patients, but still had deadly motives. On the flip side, in *The Unlucky Farmer*, the farmer did unintentionally cause harm to the people in need of food, but his heart was in the right place. The doctor strikes me as cruel, but the farmer is definitely not. So, as in the case of virtue, I lean toward saying vicious motivation is necessary for having the vices, but bad outcomes are not.

Aristotle long ago made an interesting claim about the vices: namely, that for any virtue there is at least a vice of excess and a vice of deficiency.[51] This is easier to see in some cases than others. The courageous person, for instance, is said to be in between the cowardly person (with the vice of deficiency) and the rash person (with the vice of excess).

But it is not obvious that this pattern always holds. We have to go virtue by virtue to see. Consider honesty, for instance. There is clearly a vice of deficiency, namely dishonesty. And we *say* that there can be excessive honesty. Here is an example:

> *Thomas on the Elevator.* Thomas is riding the elevator with a coworker whom he barely knows. To avoid an awkward silence, the coworker asks Thomas how his day is going. Thomas proceeds to rattle off a long list of what he has done, including what he ate for breakfast and how many times he has visited the bathroom.[52]

---

[51] For helpful discussion, see Hursthouse 1981.   [52] I develop this example in Miller 2021.

Now one *could* claim that Thomas is exhibiting the vice of excess for honesty, which would fit the pattern of Aristotle's framework. But I am not so sure that that is the right thing to say. After all, Thomas is honest to a fault. He doesn't distort the facts or in any way lie, mislead, or deceive the coworker. When it comes to just his honesty, it is hard to criticize him. Instead, we can say that the character flaw at work here is one of lacking tact or discretion. He is not sufficiently aware of or attuned to what is appropriate to communicate in this circumstance. More generally, honesty might be a virtue with a vice of deficiency, but no vice of excess. Still, to be fair to Aristotle, even if his framework does not hold in *every* case, it is useful for thinking about many virtues and how they relate to the vices.

Virtue makes up a good character, and vice a bad one. Is that all there is to character? Or could there be something in between a virtuous and a vicious character? One might say no. Some of the Stoic philosophers, for instance, held that if you fail to be virtuous you automatically are vicious. To many philosophers, though, character has more sides to it than that.

Aristotle's contributions on this issue as well have been influential. Here he actually introduced several more categories besides virtue and vice. The two that have received the most attention are continence and incontinence.[53] The continent person falls short of virtue. This person's outward behavior seems to be virtuous, but the difference lies with his underlying thoughts. The virtuous person is said to be *wholehearted*, which means that her thoughts and feelings are in alignment or harmony in doing what is right. She is not struggling with opposing temptation to lie, cheat, steal, etc., which she has to overcome in order to act well. The *continent* person, then, faces temptation to do the bad, wrestles with that temptation, and yet is able to not give into it and still acts well.

We can say the opposite of the incontinent or weak-willed person. He falls short of being vicious. The outward behavior of the incontinent person will look very similar to that of the vicious person. But here, too, the difference between them concerns what is going on in their minds, and specifically whether there is an internal motivational struggle. The vicious person shares with the virtuous person the commonality of having reason and motivation align harmoniously or wholeheartedly in favor of acting. The *incontinent* person, on the other hand, knows what the right thing to do is, but is tempted to deceive, hurt, abuse, and the like, and, when the opportunity arises, gives into that temptation.

---

[53] For additional categories, see Curzer 2012.

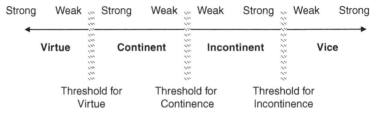

Figure 1. Central Components of Aristotle's Taxonomy of Character
Source: This figure is adapted from Miller 2017, with permission of Palgrave
Macmillan

So, the emerging picture we get from Aristotle for how to classify someone's character can be found in Figure 1. Importantly, character is malleable, and so can change over the course of one's lifespan. Even if someone starts out as incontinent when it comes to cheating, for instance, that person can improve and become continent, and even virtuous, as time goes on. Alternatively, that person's character can head in the opposite direction and become vicious instead.

While Figure 1 represents perhaps the leading taxonomy still in use today among philosophers of character, my own view is that it is unhelpful. I will briefly suggest why in Section 3.5, and offer an alternative approach.

3.3 What are the Virtues?

Thus far, our examples of virtues have mainly been compassion and honesty. I chose them on purpose, since there is likely going to be little controversy about these counting as virtues, at least among readers of this book.[54]

Nevertheless, looking beyond these two examples, it is apparent that different writers on virtue have come up with different lists of the virtues. Aristotle has his list; Aquinas, Hume, and Nietzsche each have different ones. Even if they do not always claim that their lists are exhaustive, there are conflicts with respect to particular virtues. On some lists, humility is a virtue. On other lists, it is not, and may even be considered a vice.

The abundance of such lists of virtues may encourage worries about relativism. Different lists might be equally valid, the thought could be, with no list of virtues being objectively the correct or true list. As Martha Nussbaum writes,

> The relativist, looking at different societies, is impressed by the variety and
> the apparent non-comparability in the lists of virtues she encounters.

---

[54] The next few paragraphs are adapted from Miller 2020, with permission of Routledge.

Examining the different lists, and observing the complex connections between each list and a concrete form of life and a concrete history, she may well feel that any list of virtues must be simply a reflection of local traditions and values, and that, virtues being ... concrete and closely tied to forms of life, there can in fact be no list of virtues that will serve as normative for all these varied societies.[55]

Strictly speaking, the mere existence of diverse lists does not by itself entail that moral relativism about the virtues is correct. This is no more plausible than the idea that the existence of diverse views about the shape of the Earth or the existence of God means that you must be a relativist in those domains. Diverse views can easily coexist with an objective truth about the matter.

Nevertheless, one might still worry that in the case of the virtues the *best explanation* for this diverse set of lists is that there is no fact of the matter as to what is the objectively correct list. Instead, it might seem to be a matter of individual or cultural opinion. So, while granting that there is no entailment at work here, the advocate of moral relativism still could make a case for her view being the best explanation for the diversity of the lists out there.

The challenge for those who reject moral relativism is to justify there being an objectively correct list of the virtues. Ideally, it would also be helpful to learn about what character traits are on that objective list, too.

Some progress has been made in addressing this challenge. Here, I briefly highlight two examples. One is Martha Nussbaum's classic paper, "Non-Relative Virtues: An Aristotelian Approach."[56] Claiming to largely be clarifying Aristotle's own approach, Nussbaum notes that we encounter different domains of life which "figure in more or less any human life, and in which more or less any human being will have to make *some* choices rather than others, and act in *some* way rather than some other."[57] Her examples include:

Fear of important damages, especially death
Bodily appetites and their pleasures
Distribution of limited resources.[58]

Given such domains, we then get a 'thin' account of each virtue, which will merely be "whatever it is to be stably disposed to act appropriately in that sphere."[59] Hence, there will be a virtue of acting well with respect to bodily appetites and their pleasures, although this approach won't deliver a 'thick' account of what that virtue involves.

---

[55] Nussbaum, 1988: 34.   [56] Ibid.   [57] Ibid., 35, emphasis hers.   [58] Ibid.   [59] Ibid.

Nussbaum's approach provides a nice framework for thinking about the diversity of lists of the virtues. As she writes, "People will of course disagree about what the appropriate ways of acting and reacting in fact *are*. But in that case, as Aristotle has set things up, they are arguing about the same thing, and advancing competing specifications of the same virtue. The reference of the virtue term in each case is fixed by the sphere of experience."[60]

There is much more to be said about Nussbaum's approach. But given the limitations of space, let me simply note that, if we can figure out what all the domains of life are, we may be able to justify there being a certain fixed number of virtues. Any list that is too long or too short can be criticized on this basis. On the flip side, an obvious limitation of this approach is that, even if it is sound, it would deliver only a thin account of each virtue without being able to tell us much about what those virtues look like.

A very different approach for addressing the many lists of virtues has been developed in the field of positive psychology.[61] In their mammoth volume, *Character Strengths and Virtues: A Handbook and Classification*, psychologists Christopher Peterson and Martin Seligman enlisted the help of fifty leading scholars working on character to come up with a new taxonomy for what they called the 'character strengths.'[62]

Their approach was richly empirical and cross-cultural. They looked to writings from traditions as diverse as Confucianism, Buddhism, ancient Greek philosophy, and medieval Islam. They put together the traits mentioned favorably by Charlemagne, Benjamin Franklin, the Boy and Girl Scouts, Hallmark greeting cards, Pokémon characters, and many other sources.[63] With such a large number of possible character strengths to work with, they needed to come up with a procedure to help winnow them down. Here are the ten criteria they used, which I have simplified a bit to make them easier to grasp:[64]

(1) A strength contributes to the good life for oneself and for others.
(2) Each strength is morally valued intrinsically or for its own sake, and not just because of the good effects it might have on the world.
(3) The display of a strength by one person does not diminish other people's strengths.

---

[60] Ibid., 36, emphasis hers.
[61] What follows is based very loosely on Miller 2019a, with permission of Taylor and Francis.
[62] Peterson and Seligman 2004.   [63] Ibid., 15, 33–52.   [64] Ibid., 17–27.

(4) If it is it easy to come up with an opposite of an alleged character strength that is a pleasant trait, this counts against regarding it as a genuine character strength.[65]

(5) It should have a degree of generality across situations and stability across time.

(6) The strength is distinct from other strengths in the classification.

(7) The character strength is embodied in people who are exemplars or role models of the strength.

(8) We do not believe that this feature can be applied to all strengths, but an additional criterion where sensible is the existence of prodigies or humans who are very high on the strength at an early age.[66]

(9) Conversely, another criterion for a character strength is the existence of people who show – selectively – the total absence of a given strength.

(10) The larger society provides institutions and associated rituals for cultivating the strength and then for sustaining its practice.

To make the final cut, a character strength did not need to meet all these criteria, just 'most' of them.[67]

The result was a list of twenty-four character strengths, which were organized into six categories and became known as the "Values in Action" or VIA classification.[68] Table 1 shows the categories in bold in the left-hand column and the character strengths in the remaining columns. The *Handbook* then proceeded to offer a detailed discussion of each of these twenty-four character strengths.

While there are problems with their approach,[69] Peterson and Seligman are to be commended for the tremendous amount of work they put into trying to find an empirically grounded taxonomy of character strengths, or what I would simply call 'virtues.'

3.4 The Negative Empirical Story: Lack of Virtue?

It is one thing to know what the virtues are in theory. It is another thing to actually possess them as part of one's character. Are the virtues widely held by most people today? To help with this question, let's turn to some more of the relevant empirical research in psychology.

One of my favorite studies of all time was conducted by Robert Baron. Baron observed whether shoppers in a mall would perform a simple helping task. Shoppers in the control condition had just passed a clothing store and then had

---

[65] I must confess that I have never been able to understand this criterion very well.

[66] Like number 4, this one has also always puzzled me.   [67] Ibid., 16.   [68] Ibid., 29–30.

[69] For my own criticisms, see Miller 2019a.

Table 1 The 24 Character Strengths from Positive Psychology

Wisdom	Creativity	Curiosity	Open-Mindedness	Love of Learning	Perspective
Courage	Bravery	Persistence	Integrity	Vitality	
Humanity	Love	Kindness	Social Intelligence		
Justice	Citizenship	Fairness	Leadership		
Temperance	Forgiveness and Mercy	Humility/ Modesty	Prudence	Self-Regulation	
Transcendence	Appreciation of Beauty and Excellence	Gratitude	Hope	Humor	Spirituality

a chance to help. Shoppers in a second group had just passed a different kind of store (to be revealed in a moment), and then had the same chance to help. Here was the difference in helping between the two groups:

	First location	**Second location**
Males Helping	22%	45%
Females Helping	17%	61%

The second store must have had something to do with charity or nonprofit work, right? Actually it was Mrs. Fields Cookies or Cinnabon.[70]

Studies such as Baron's have received a fair amount of attention in the recent philosophy literature on character. The leading contributors here have been Gilbert Harman, in a series of papers dating back to 1999; and John Doris, in several papers and, most importantly, in his 2002 book, *Lack of Character: Personality and Moral Behavior.*[71] Broadly speaking, their reasoning goes as follows:

---

[70] See Baron 1997.
[71] Harman 1999, 2000, 2001, 2003, 2009, Doris 1998, 2002, 2010, and Merritt et al. 2010. See also Alfano 2013.

(1) If there is widespread possession of the traditional virtues, then empirical observations using relevant psychology experiments will find most people behaving in a certain kind of way.

(2) However, empirical observations using relevant psychology experiments fail to find that most people act in this kind of way.

(3) Therefore, there is not widespread possession of the traditional virtues.[72]

Here are three additional examples of studies which have occupied a central place in this discussion in philosophy:

Dime in the Phone Booth. The psychologists Isen and Levin had an experimental group find a dime in the coin return slot of a phone booth, whereas the control group did not. Later on, individuals in both groups subsequently had a chance to help pick up dropped papers. The question was whether the presence or absence of the dime earlier made any difference to their willingness to help. It did: 88% of those who found a dime helped, but only 4% of those who did not find a dime helped.[73] There were replication problems with this study, but there are many other studies on the effect of mood on helping which found a similar pattern.[74]

Lady in Distress. In the 1969 "Lady in Distress" experiment, participants heard a loud crash in the next room together with a woman's scream. It sounded like a bookshelf had toppled down on her, and cries of pain quickly followed. The question was whether participants would do anything to help. Those who were by themselves helped 70% of the time. But surprisingly, if a participant was in the same room with a stranger who didn't do anything to respond, helping happened only 7% of the time.[75]

Obedience to Authority. Stanley Milgram's shock experiments are arguably the most famous in the history of psychology. Especially relevant is experiment five, wherein a participant had to give a test to an innocent person in another room, and turn up a dial with what they thought were increasingly greater shocks for each wrong answer. At 270 volts, the test taker demanded to be released from the test and was making agonizing screams. At higher levels the pleas became desperate and hysterical. Nevertheless, under pressure from an authority figure, 80% of participants went at least to 270 volts, and 65% went all the way to the 450 volt level labeled 'XXX,' which was a lethal level of shock (so they thought).[76]

Other studies which are often cited include the Princeton Theological Seminary hurry study and the Stanford prison experiment.[77]

---

[72] For more, see Doris 1998: 505–507, and Merritt et al. 2010: 357–358.

[73] Isen and Levin 1972.   [74] See Miller 2013 for details.

[75] Latané and Rodin 1969: 193–195, and Latané and Darley 1970: 60–63.

[76] Milgram 1974: 60.   [77] See Darley and Batson 1973 and Haney et al. 1973, respectively.

Note that all these studies are connected to helping, and so Harman and Doris are thereby focusing on the empirical reality of just one virtue, namely compassion. This focus made a great deal of sense. There are numerous studies that have been done over the past sixty years on helping behavior, in contrast to the smaller number of studies of behavior which might pertain to other virtues. Nevertheless, Harman and Doris did not take the conclusion of their argument to apply just to one virtue, and so expected that future studies in other areas of morality will tell a similar story about absent virtue. I have also looked extensively at the literature on helping, but branched out into empirical research on cheating and lying as well.[78]

To return to the main argument, how are these helping studies supposed to tell against the widespread possession of the virtue of compassion? It isn't as simple as showing that people behaved less than virtuously in the various experimental situations. After all, when participants found a dime, or when participants were alone in the next room, they *did* tend to help. Same thing with the smell from Mrs. Fields Cookies and Cinnabon. In another version of the Milgram setup, when participants at the 150 volt level heard commands from two authority figures which contradicted each other, they immediately stopped at that level or one more level above it.[79]

Rather, the alleged conflict with the virtue of compassion stems from the apparent failure of most participants to be appropriately sensitive to the morally relevant considerations. A compassionate person would not help in a way that is so sensitive to finding a dime, the smell of cookies, or the presence of an unresponsive bystander. Nor would a compassionate person be so *in*sensitive to the screams and eventual death of a test taker. As Harman and Doris wrote, "both disappointing omissions and appalling actions are *readily* induced through seemingly minor situations. What makes these findings so striking is just how *insubstantial* the situational influences that produce troubling moral failures seem to be."[80]

In my own work, I have tried to clarify in more detail a number of ways in which the results from the empirical research seem to be at odds with the widespread possession of compassion.[81] Here I will just mention a couple of examples. First, it seems clear that:

---

[78] See Miller 2013, 2014, 2021.   [79] Milgram 1974: 95, 105–107.

[80] Merritt et al. 2010: 357, emphasis theirs. See also Doris 1998: 507, 2002: 2, 28, 35–36; Harman 2003: 90.

[81] See Miller 2013, 2014. See also Alfano 2013.

(a) A person who is compassionate, when acting in character, will typically attempt to help when, at the very least, the need for help is obvious and the effort involved in helping is very minimal.

But in many studies we find at least one group that helps very little, such as in *Lady in Distress* and in Baron's study. Second,

(b) A compassionate person's trait of compassion will not be dependent on the presence of certain factors such as moderate guilt, embarrassment, or a good mood in leading her to perform helpful actions, such that if these factors were not present, then her frequency of helping would significantly decrease in the same situations.

In other words, a compassionate person should reliably help when in a good mood, but *also* reliably help when not in a good mood. But numerous studies, such as Baron's, find that guilt relief, embarrassment relief, and maintaining a good mood are significant factors impacting helping.[82] On the flip side,

(c) A compassionate person's trait of compassion will not be dependent on the absence of certain factors such as anticipated moderate embarrassment or blame, or moderately bad moods that inhibit her from performing helpful actions, such that if these factors were not present, then her frequency of helping would significantly increase in the same situations.

Again, plenty of studies suggest that factors such as the avoidance of embarrassment (as in *Lady in Distress*) and blame, and the presence of a negative mood, do significantly decrease people's helping behavior.[83]

There are other criteria for compassion that could be mentioned here. Rather than continue down this path, it is also important to step back and be clear about what exactly the conclusion is that people such as Harman, Doris, and myself are drawing.[84] It is not the very strong empirical claim that:

(i) No human being has ever had any of the traditional virtues such as compassion.

In fact, as far as the studies themselves found, they do not rule out there being a few virtuous and a few vicious people.[85]

---

[82] For a review of some of these findings, see Miller 2013: chapters two and three.

[83] See ibid., chapter six.

[84] Here I follow Miller 2014: 193–194, with permission of Oxford University Press.

[85] Doris 2002: 60, 65, 112, 122.

At the same time, it would be too weak to just say this:

(ii) Given the psychological evidence, we are not justified in believing on the basis of that evidence that most people possess the traditional virtues such as compassion.

This is an expression of ignorance, and does not take a stand on whether most people possess the traditional virtues. Instead, here is how the conclusion should be understood:

(iii) Given the psychological evidence, we are justified in believing on the basis of that evidence that most people *do not* possess the traditional virtues such as compassion.[86]

This claim definitely does take a stand. At the same time, it is not claiming certainty, but rather is defeasible and so could be overturned by future studies. But for now it looks to be well supported.

Admittedly, not everyone has been convinced to draw the same conclusion. While there have been a number of critiques offered of the case for (iii), given limitations of space I will just highlight one. Perhaps the results of the relevant studies are best interpreted not as supporting a conclusion about lack of virtue, but rather as suggesting the contribution of *competing* virtues. For instance, instead of saying that the standard Milgram experiment is evidence that most participants did not have the virtue of compassion, perhaps a better interpretation is to say that their compassion was being outweighed by the work of another virtue which seemed at the time to have greater priority. One candidate for this virtue could be obedience. Or take the *Lady in Distress* study. Here again participants might have had their compassion outweighed by another virtue, such as trust, as they followed the example of the other person in the room who did not respond. Additional candidates for competing virtues might be found for the other studies that get mentioned in this debate.[87]

3.5 The Positive Empirical Story: What is the Best One?

Nevertheless, suppose we grant that most people do not possess the traditional virtues. Indeed, I bet many of us are already inclined to

---

[86] Hence, Doris argues that "people typically lack character" (Doris 1998: 506, 2002: 2). In a coauthored article along with Maria Merritt, Harman and Doris together say that, "Behavior is *not* typically ordered by robust traits" (Merritt et al. 2010: 358, emphasis theirs).

[87] For discussion see Solomon 2003: 53, 55–56, and Kristjánsson 2008: 64–65.

think this way, even before we come across the empirical literature. Human history, world events, and the teachings of various religions could lead to a similar conclusion. In fact, both Plato and Aristotle accepted it long ago.

Saying that most of us lack the traditional virtues is a negative claim about what we are *not* like. Far less attention has been paid by philosophers to developing the best positive story of what our character *is* like. These seem to be the leading contenders at the moment:

(i) Most people have the vices, such as dishonesty and cowardice. I, along with Harman and Doris, have claimed that this position also does not fit the empirical data, but not everyone agrees.[88]

(ii) Most people have local character traits, which are virtues and vices restricted to narrow types of situations such as the courtroom or the bar. Someone might have honesty just in test-taking situations, while not having honesty in courtrooms. Harman seems to be amenable to this position, and Doris explicitly accepts it.[89]

(iii) Most people have characters which are continent. Or, most people have characters which are incontinent and hence they typically suffer from weakness of will. I am not aware of any philosophers today who have defended these options.

(iv) Most people have mixed character traits, which are cross-situationally consistent traits that are neither good enough to qualify as virtues nor bad enough to qualify as vices. They are made up of some morally positive and some morally negative psychological features. I have developed this position at length.[90]

Let me say very briefly why I do not accept the first three options, before expanding on the last one.

It will help to return to Baron's study of helping in the shopping mall. Why did the smell from Mrs. Field's Cookies and Cinnabon have such a big impact? We do not know for sure, but one leading explanation goes like this: The good smell put nearby shoppers in a good mood. This in turn activated a desire to maintain that good mood. A lot of things could keep the good mood going, one of which is the satisfaction we get from helping others. Lo and behold, here

---

[88] Bates and Kleingeld 2018.   [89] Doris 1998: 507–508, 2002: 23, 25, 64.
[90] Miller 2013, 2014.

comes an opportunity to help. Hence, the shopper is motivated more so than usual to help.

Suppose this story is along the right lines for explaining the data. In that case, one thing to note is that it does not seem to be a story we would expect if most of the shoppers had possessed the vice of apathy, which is what corresponds to the virtue of compassion. In other words, I would not expect an apathetic person's helping to significantly increase based on the presence of pleasant fragrances. Additional surprising results for widespread apathy include that the majority of participants helped when alone in *Lady in Distress*, and that the majority of participants did not give severe shocks in versions of the Milgram studies where no authority figure was present or multiple authority figures contradicted each other.

The story we have told about Baron's study helps illustrate why positing local character traits is no help either. The desire to maintain a good mood is what is doing the work in explaining the increased helping in the smell situation. But this desire is not limited to shopping malls or Mrs. Field's Cookies. It can be activated and function in a *wide variety* of different situations. The same is true for our fear of embarrassment (central to explaining the effect of being with unresponsive strangers), our obedience to authority (central to explaining Milgram's findings), and a host of other psychological dispositions which emerge in the empirical literature, such as desires to alleviate a negative mood or eliminate feelings of guilt or embarrassment. They are all robustly cross-situationally consistent.

Finally, continence and incontinence do not do the job either. On the same grounds that we can doubt widespread virtue, we do not see a consistent pattern of good moral behavior across the studies. But on the same grounds that we can doubt widespread vice, we do not see a consistent pattern of bad moral behavior across the studies either. Rather, our behavior seems like it is very much a mixed bag.

Enter mixed character traits. The claim is that rather than compassion, most of us have a mixed helping trait. Rather than honesty, most of us have a mixed cheating trait. And so on. They have some positive aspects to them. For instance, a mixed helping trait will give rise to helping behavior in certain circumstances, such as when the helping is seen as an opportunity to maintain a good mood. But it will not do so in other circumstances, such as when the very same helping task might lead to feelings of embarrassment.

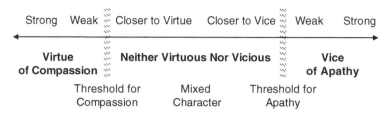

Figure 2. Compassion, Mixed Helping Trait, and Apathy
Source: This figure is adapted from Miller 2017, with permission of Palgrave Macmillan.

This mixed bag applies to motivation as well. As we said, the virtue of compassion requires altruistic motivation, which, given Batson's empathy-altruism hypothesis, is likely tied to empathy. A mixed helping trait includes empathetic capacities, which is one of the reasons why it is not a vice. But it also includes motives to, say, help in order to maintain a good mood. In other words, egoistic motives for helping are present too and will likely be influential. That is one of the reasons why it is not a virtue.

With a mixed trait picture, the taxonomy of character traits looks something like Figure 2, with compassion as the representative virtue. Note that continence and incontinence are not in the picture. Compassion and apathy come in degrees, but so does the mixed-helping trait. And even if we happen to have such a mixed trait, we are not stuck with it and can gradually make progress in either direction.

Much more could be said about both the negative empirical story of lack of virtue and the positive story about mixed traits.[91] This will have to suffice for now.

4 Moral Judgment and Motivation: Motivational Internalism and Impossibilities of Our Wills

Franklin decides to go visit Sally in the hospital. He judges that to be the right thing to do. Let us now add to our story that Franklin is a compassionate person, and that his judgment arose from his compassionate character. Then, given the claims made in previous sections, we know that Franklin isn't always motivated to pursue his own self-interest, and so psychological egoism is false, at least in this case. Furthermore, we know he is ultimately motivated altruistically to be with Sally out of genuine concern for her, independently of how he might benefit. His virtuous character, including his altruistic motivation to help her, led to the formation of his judgment that visiting her is the right thing to do.

---

[91] See Miller 2013, 2014, 2021.

Our character traits, including our ultimate motives for action, play a central role in shaping the specific moral judgments we make. In the remaining sections of this Element, our focus will turn to those moral judgments we form on a daily basis. To begin, in this section we will look at the debate surrounding whether our moral judgments always motivate us to act. As we will see, there are various reasons to be skeptical that they do. One of those reasons has to do with the impossibilities of our wills, a concept which will be the other main topic of this section.[92]

4.1 Introducing Motivational Internalism

When Franklin formed his moral judgment to visit Sally, it led him to be motivated to visit her. But did it *have* to motivate him? According to the position known as *motivational internalism*, the answer is yes, it did. Otherwise it would not have counted as a genuine moral judgment in the first place.

There is a lot of intuitive plausibility to the idea that our moral judgments always motivate us to some extent. Suppose Franklin is talking to his friend Lionel, and Lionel asks him what he is going to do next. Franklin replies:

"I should go visit Sally in the hospital now."

Yet Franklin does not make any attempt to get off the couch in Lionel's apartment. Lionel assumes that this must be because something more important has now crossed Franklin's mind, leading him to delay the visit. When pressed about why he isn't going, though, Franklin replies:

"No, there is nothing else I should do instead that is more important, but I just don't have any motivation to visit Sally."

Lionel might rightly be puzzled at this point. He could wonder whether Franklin really made a genuine moral judgment in the first place. Maybe Franklin was just making a "moral judgment" in name only. This reaction is just what you would expect if motivational internalism were true.

Although there are different ways to formulate the view, we will use the following as our official statement of motivational internalism for the purposes of this section:

(MI) Necessarily, if any person judges that some available action is morally right for her to perform or refrain from performing, then that person is motivated at least to some extent to perform or refrain from performing that action.

---

[92] The remainder of this section is adapted from Miller 2008a, with permission of Springer.

Several things are worth unpacking here.

First, 'necessarily' means that it is simply impossible to make a genuine moral judgment and not be motivated accordingly. This is supposed to be understood as a conceptual truth, telling us something important about how our concept of moral judgment works. If we find that someone is not motivated at all to act a certain way, then we can conclude that the person never judged it to be morally right to do in the first place.

Second, the person only needs to be motivated 'to some extent.' This is not the same thing as saying that the person necessarily has to *do* what she judges to be right. She might judge making a donation to the charity Oxfam to be morally right, be motivated to do so, but give in to temptation and play video games instead. The motivation, in other words, can be defeasible.

The opposing position, *motivational externalism*, should come as no surprise. It says that it is conceptually *possible* to make a genuine moral judgment and not be motivated at all by that judgment. So, if you find that someone is not motivated to do something, by itself that would not guarantee the absence of a moral judgment.

Why does this debate matter? For one thing, if motivational internalism is true, then it sheds a lot of light on what is involved in making a moral judgment. We would know that moral judgments have to be motivating, or at the very least give rise to motivation. That could lead us to think of moral judgments more along the lines of desires, rather than beliefs. As we will see in the next section, this line of reasoning will factor into a very influential argument in meta-ethics.

4.2 Evaluating Motivational Internalism

Is motivational internalism, as understood in (MI), even true? Is it simply impossible to make a moral judgment and not be motivated at least to some extent? There seems to be a great deal of consensus among philosophers that it is possible for moral judgments to leave us cold. Here, I briefly mention a few of the influential examples that have been raised by motivational externalists:

> *Moral Rebels and Sadists.* James Dreier gives us the case of the Sadists who will say things like "We despise what is good because it is good. We believe the things you say are good are in fact, and we are never motivated to promote those things. Quite the opposite!"[93]
>
> *Depression and Listlessness.* Here is a case from Al Mele: "Consider an unfortunate person ... who is suffering from clinical depression because of the recent tragic deaths of her husband and children in a plane crash. *Seemingly*, we can imagine that she retains some of her beliefs that she is

---

[93] Dreier 1990: 10–11.

morally required to do certain things … while being utterly devoid of motivation to act accordingly. "[94]

Psychopaths. Valerie Tiberius notes that "it seems possible for there to be a true amoralist who sincerely judges that it is morally wrong to murder someone, for example, but has no disposition to be moved by this whatsoever. Philosophers have traditionally imagined amoralists, but now we have evidence of real people who might fit the bill, namely, psychopaths."[95]

Time Passing. Here is a case from Connie Rosati: "Perhaps she judges that she morally ought to work actively to aid the sick and poor. After 20 years of doing so, she concludes that she has done enough and ceases to be motivated to act on her judgment, yet she continues to judge that she morally ought to work actively to aid the sick and poor. Doesn't it seem plausible that she is competent with the moral concepts, that she speaks sincerely."[96]

In response, motivational internalists have raised challenges to certain of these examples, and it is fair to say that some of them might be more persuasive than others. Nevertheless, because of examples like those above, today it is generally agreed by all sides that internalism as formulated in (MI) is false.

That does not end the discussion, however. For in place of (MI), internalists have developed various *restricted* versions of the view. These are intended to avoid the counterexamples listed above, by narrowing the scope of internalism to a select group of people, such as those who are rational or who are virtuous. We will unpack these variations in a moment. First, let me introduce a new kind of counterexample of my own, and in so doing take a look at another fascinating side of our moral psychology.

4.3 Volitional Impossibility and Motivational Internalism

Consider the following examples:

The Soldier. A soldier believes that were he to flee the scene of the battle at this very moment, he almost certainly would be able to emerge from the conflict unharmed. But he finds it simply unthinkable that he abandon the other members of his platoon, even though there is considerable risk to his well-being as a result of remaining in the engagement.

The Guard. A guard is ordered to take the family members of a political prisoner and execute them without attracting any attention in the process. The guard sincerely believes that he ought to carry out these orders in virtue of his allegiance to the state, and yet when it comes time to actually pull the trigger, he is overwhelmed by the innocence of the prisoner's children and the horrendous nature of the act he is about to perform. As a result, he comes to believe that he is incapable of carrying out the order.

---

[94] Mele 2003: 111, emphasis in original. See also Stocker 1979; Smith 1994: 61, 120, 135–136; Dreier 1990: 10; Svavarsdóttir 1999: 164–165; and Shafer-Landau 2003b: 150.
[95] Tiberius 2015: 80. See also Roskies 2003.   [96] Rosati 2016.

These cases center around something that was impossible for the soldier and for the guard. While they were actions which they physically could perform, in a deeper sense they could not bring themselves to do them. They were morally unthinkable. These are examples of *volitional impossibilities* or impossibilities of our wills.

Saying that the soldier did not want to leave his fellow troops is not enough to capture what is going on. Sometimes we cannot do something because of a desire which we do not endorse, such as a strong addiction or a debilitating phobia. These forces may not be a part of our will. Yet the soldier in our example is fully behind his decision not to run away, rather than being compelled to remain by a desire beyond his control which he does not endorse. As Harry Frankfurt, one of the leading contributors to understanding volitional impossibility, writes:

> Being unable to bring oneself to perform an action is not the same as simply being overwhelmingly averse to performing it ... In addition, *the aversion has his endorsement; and it constrains his conduct so effectively precisely because of this.* The person's endorsement of his aversion is what distinguishes situations in which someone finds an action unthinkable from those in which an inability to act is due to addiction or to some other type of irresistible impulse.[97]

Thus, as a first pass we can characterize volitional impossibility this way:

(VI) It is *volitionally impossible* for a person to perform a given action if and only if psychologically the person is strongly averse to doing the action, and she also endorses this aversion.

For our purposes, we won't try to spell out what 'endorsement' amounts to. This is a huge topic in the philosophy of action, with Frankfurt himself having made a number of influential contributions.

It seems to me that cases of volitional impossibility could cause trouble for motivational internalism. Here is how this might happen:

(1) Possibly, a person judges that her acting a certain way is morally right for her to do (or refrain from doing), but she is also overwhelmingly averse to doing the action, and endorses that aversion. Hence, the action is volitionally impossible for her.

But now suppose this is true:

(2) If it is volitionally impossible for someone to perform an action at a given time, then the person is not motivated to do the action at that time.

Together these can lead us to conclude that:

---

[97] Frankfurt 1988: 182, emphasis mine. See also Frankfurt 1993: 112.

(3) Possibly, a person can make a moral judgment that an action is right for her
     to perform, and yet not be motivated to do it.

In other words, motivational externalism is true.

This is abstract, so let's take an example. Perhaps the best known case of
volitional impossibility in the recent philosophical literature is the following
from Frankfurt:

> Consider a mother who reaches the conclusion, after conscientious deliber-
> ation, that it would be best for her to give up her child for adoption, and
> suppose that she decides to do so. When the moment arrives for actually
> giving up the child, however, she may find that she cannot go through with it –
> not because she has reconsidered the matter and changed her mind but
> because she simply cannot bring herself to give her child away.[98]

Here is one way of unpacking this story further. Initially the mother believes
that, in light of the relevant considerations, it would be morally best for her to
give her child up for adoption. When the time comes, the mother still thinks that
it would be *morally* best for her to give her child up for adoption, but it would
not be best *all things considered* for her to give her child up for adoption.

Frankfurt himself further develops his case along these lines:

> [The mother] may recognize her discovery as a revelation not just of the fact
> that keeping the child is what is most important to her, but also of the deeper
> fact that it is what she truly wants to be most important to her. In [this] case,
> she is glad to be putting her need for the relationship above what is best by
> a measure that she now refuses to regard as decisive.[99]

The mother has undergone a fundamental shift in the degree to which she cares
about doing what is morally right on the one hand and her relationship with the
child on the other.

Hence, this is a case not of a conflicted will, but of volitional impossibility. By
having to actually hand her daughter over, the mother has discovered the fundamental importance that her daughter holds in her life, and furthermore she wants
her child to have that importance. This new-found depth of care for her daughter
causes the mother to fully align herself with keeping the child, while being averse
to turning over her child – an aversion which she fully endorses.

Thus, it is volitionally impossible for the mother to give her child away. As
such it would be odd to say that she is still motivated to do so. She is fully behind
her aversion to parting with her child. Yet at the same time she still has her moral
judgment. Hence, motivational internalism as captured by (MI) is false.

---

[98] Frankfurt 1993: 111.   [99] See Frankfurt 2002: 163.

4.4 Volitional Impossibility and Normal People

According to the philosopher James Dreier, traditional motivational internalism as stated in (MI) is false because of cases involving moral rebels and people suffering from depression, two of the examples we saw in Section 4.2.[100] But he claims that this result is compatible with a more modest form of internalism which endorses the principle that, "in normal contexts a person has some motivation to promote what he believes to be good."[101] Unfortunately, Dreier admits that he has little to say in terms of characterizing what makes a context or person 'normal.'[102]

Regardless of how we pin down the sense of 'normal' in question, it is hard to see how, in Frankfurt's example, the mother's circumstances or her inability to be moved by her moral judgment are abnormal in any relevant sense. For instance, the possession of what may have been a *false* moral belief about it being best to give up her child for adoption is no sign of abnormality.

Another contemporary philosopher, Sigrún Svavarsdóttir, makes a similar proposal on behalf of the motivational internalist. According to her, motivational internalism is the thesis that "moral judgements are of conceptual necessity connected to motivation to pursue or promote what is judged favorably and to shun or prevent what is judged unfavorably, except in individuals suffering from motivational disorders that affect them more generally."[103] Svavarsdóttir builds in this exception clause because she thinks that counterexamples to motivational internalism involving emotional depression, listlessness, and the like are convincing.[104] However, this does not help with examples involving volitional impossibility, since they do not have to involve people suffering from general motivational disorders of any kind.

As things now stand, this first attempt at giving a plausible restricted formulation of motivational internalism also does not seem to be immune to our counterexample.

4.5 Volitional Impossibility and Subjectively Rational People

Somewhat more promising in my view is to restrict motivational internalism to rational people:

(RMI) Necessarily, if any person judges that some available action is morally right for her to perform or refrain from performing, then either (i) that person

---

[100] Dreier 1990: 10–11.   [101] Ibid., 14.   [102] For some details, see ibid., 11–13.

[103] See Svavarsdóttir 1999: 165. Svavarsdóttir herself rejects even this restricted form of motivational internalism because of her own counterexamples (176–183).

[104] Ibid., 163–164.

is motivated at least to some extent to perform or refrain from performing that action, or (ii) she is practically irrational.[105]

Practical rationality in turn can be understood in a subjective or an objective way. On the first view, practical rationality is a matter of proper responsiveness to the practical reasons there are *from the person's own perspective*. Hence, if I drink a glass of clear water that came from the sink, I am being rational even if, unbeknownst to me, the water line had been contaminated two minutes earlier. On the other hand, objective rationality typically requires that one's actions mirror the reasons *there really are* for behaving a certain way. In the contaminated water case, then, I am being objectively irrational even though I do not know that the water is hazardous, since I have no reason to drink contaminated water.

We do not have to pick between subjective and objective approaches to practical rationality. Let's just consider each one in turn. So, we can start by taking (RMI) and, for the words "practically irrational," we can understand them in the *subjective* way we have just clarified. Hence, someone who makes a moral judgment but is *not* motivated at all to do what it says is being irrational from his own perspective. He is failing to be responsive to what he can see he has reason to do – namely, the action he judges to be right.

Volitional impossibility cases will be a problem for this position. The mother in our example is fully behind not giving her child up for adoption. She is in alignment with her reasons for action as she sees them. So she is both rational (subjectively) and not motivated to part from her child. That is the exact opposite of what the subjective version of (RMI) would say.

4.6 Volitional Impossibility and Objectively Rational People

What about if we replace rationality from a person's perspective with objective rationality in (RMI)? We would be saying that either a person is motivated by his moral judgments or he is irrational because he is failing to be responsive to the correct reasons there really are which govern his behavior. So, now our question becomes: must it *always* be the case that someone who makes a moral judgment either is motivated or fails to conform to what she has most reason to do?

Not obviously, I would say. Consider cases of volitional impossibility where the moral judgment to perform some action is *false*. Then it is a good thing that she does not perform the action. She has no objective reason to, and plenty of

---

[105] For development of such a view, see Smith 1994.

reason not to. Here is a modification of Frankfurt's case which fits this description:

> Consider a mother who reaches the conclusion, after conscientious deliber-
> ation and as a result of the indoctrination which she has received as a member
> of her cult, that it would be morally best for her to sacrificially kill her child
> for the good of the cause. Suppose she decides to do so. When the moment
> arrives for actually murdering her child, however, she may find that she
> cannot go through with it. This is not because she has reconsidered the matter
> and changed her mind about what morality requires from her perspective, but
> simply because she cannot bring herself to kill her child. At the same time,
> she experiences this inability as liberating and as an expression of who she
> truly is as a person.

In this case, then, it was the mother's inability which preserved her practical rationality. Thus, ironically we actually get the opposite result from that intended by (RMI). Were it to turn out that the mother *is* motivated to act in accordance with her moral judgment, then in that respect she would be practically *irrational*.

Therefore, even a restricted version of motivational internalism like (RMI) that uses an objective theory of rationality is problematic. There are cases where someone might make a moral judgment, not be motivated at all by it, and yet *also be practically rational in an objective sense*.

4.7 Volitional Impossibility and Virtuous People

Finally, let us briefly turn to a third approach that the restricted motivational internalist might be tempted to employ. While motivational internalism may well be false as a conceptual claim about normal people and rational people, perhaps it is true of the *virtuous*.[106] More precisely, perhaps the following is true:

(VMI) Necessarily, if any person judges that some available action is morally right for her to perform or refrain from performing and that person is virtuous, then she is motivated at least to some extent to perform or refrain from performing that action.

Talk of 'virtuous people' here connects back to our earlier section on character and virtue.

What should we make of (VMI)? Now at last we have arrived at a claim that seems highly plausible. I simply cannot imagine a situation in which, for example, a fully courageous person would judge that it is a requirement of

---

[106] For development of such a view, see McDowell 1978.

courage for him to perform an action, but not be motivated at least to some extent to perform it. Similarly, we may have reached the limits of the volitional impossibility counterexamples. It seems unlikely that a virtuous person would find it impossible to do something that he has rightly figured out is morally required.

Keep in mind, though, that (VMI) is a far cry from our starting point with unrestricted (MI). While traditionally motivational internalism was intended to be a claim about all people, now it is only true of the highly selective class of the highly virtuous. Also, (VMI) derives its apparent plausibility from what is packed into being a 'virtuous person' in the first place. A virtuous person is one who does the virtuous thing from a virtuous state of character. And doing the virtuous thing in a virtuous way entails being motivated to do the virtuous thing. So (VMI) may well be true simply because we understand 'virtuous people' in part as those who are motivated at least to some extent to do what they judge to be required of them. That hardly makes for a very interesting internalist claim.

What we can conclude from this extended examination of various formulations of motivational internalism is, I think, the following. The burden of proof now rests with internalists to come up with a statement of their view which meets two criteria: (i) it is philosophically interesting, and (ii) it is immune to the various counterexamples that have been developed, volitional impossibility cases among them.

5 What Motivates Us? Humean and Anti-Humean Theories of Motivation

Even if it turns out that there are certain cases where we make a moral judgment but are not motivated at all to do what it says, they are surely the exception and not the rule. Most of the time we are motivated by what we judge is right to do, and at least some of the time that motivation is strong enough to give rise to action. In our central example, Franklin's decision that he should visit Sally in the hospital led to a series of subsequent motives which ended up with his walking through the door to her room.

In this section, we will probe in more detail what exactly it is that motivates us to act, especially when it comes to moral matters. On the leading position defended by a number of philosophers, the so-called Humean theory of motivation, the answer is that it is our *desires* which are what motivate us. The main rival position holds that sometimes our *beliefs* can motivate us to act. We will first explore what this debate is about and why it is important, followed by a quick review of some of the leading arguments for the Humean theory. We will end, however, by considering whether in fact it is *neither* our beliefs *nor* our desires which are what motivate us.[107]

5.1 What is the Humean Theory of Motivation?

Unfortunately, it is not an easy matter to formulate the Humean theory of motivation, as philosophers have stated it in many different ways in recent years.[108] However, there seems to be some common ground among Humeans:

> *The Desire Thesis*: In order for a person to be motivated to perform a particular action, the person must have a desire to perform the action.

Humeans often understand the sense of 'desire' loosely, just as we did in Section 1. This sense includes a wide variety of states with a world-to-mind direction of fit, such as wants, drives, wishes, impulses, likes, and so on.

While perhaps necessary, the Desire Thesis is clearly not sufficient for being a Humean about motivation, as it only requires that a desire be *present* in a person's psychology in order for her to be motivated. But the Humean wants to say more – namely, that the desire is the *source* of that motivation and is what motivates the action.

Another way to clarify this is to note that Anti-Humeans (advocates of the opposing position) could also agree that desires have to be present for motivation to occur.[109] But this is compatible with saying that *beliefs* are what motivate action. That is something that no Humean is willing to accept.

So, what needs to be added to the Desire Thesis to get a distinctive Humean theory of motivation? There are different answers in the philosophy literature, but to keep things simple let's just go with this one:

> The *Humean theory of motivation* holds that in order for a person to be motivated to perform a particular action, the person must have a desire to perform the action, and that desire by itself must be what motivates the person to act.[110]

---

[107] This section loosely draws from Miller 2008b, with permission of Wiley-Blackwell.

[108] In formulating the Humean theory, I have been helped by Smith 1994: chapter four, and Cuneo 2002. Despite its name, advocates of the theory make no claim to be accurately representing Hume's own view.

[109] This has been widely acknowledged by both Humeans and anti-Humeans alike. See, for example, Dancy 2000: 13–14, 85, 90, 94, and Smith 1994: 93.

[110] See Collins 1988: 333, and Svavarsdóttir 1999: 168. Some Humeans might complain that this is still not enough, since it would allow that desires which motivate action could be *causally generated* by one or more beliefs. Since that might make it seem like it is ultimately the relevant beliefs and not the desires which are doing the motivating, some philosophers have insisted that the desires in question also be causally independent (see, for example, the discussion in Cuneo 2002: 467). Fortunately, for our purposes we do not have to try to sort out the best formulation of the Humean theory.

With this in mind, we can switch to the other side and clarify what the Anti-Humean maintains.

Clearly, one way to be an Anti-Humean is to just reject the Desire Thesis. So this would in effect be saying:

> In order for a person to be motivated to perform a particular action, the person does not need to have a desire to perform the action.

But now we have also seen a second way to reject the Humean theory, which is to say that:

> A desire to perform the action must be present, but by itself it does not have to be what motivates the person to act.

As an alternative, the Anti-Humean highlights how *beliefs* can play a role in motivation. In other words, for the Anti-Humean it is possible for someone to be motivated by a belief *without* desiring to perform an action, or, if a desire must be present, it is nevertheless the belief which is what motivates the person to act. For instance, perhaps I can form the belief that an action is good or right to do, and have that motivate me to act, independently of any contribution from a desire to do so. Or, if a desire must be present, it is still the moral belief which is the source of the motivation.

We won't weigh in on this dispute between Humeans and Anti-Humeans about motivation for now, but will return to it in Section 5.4.

5.2 Why Should We Care?

Figuring out the role of beliefs and desires in motivation may be interesting in its own right. But does it have any larger significance for debates in moral philosophy? It does indeed. Here I will mention only one such debate, given limitations of space.[111] It has to do with what I call the Motivation Argument.

The Motivation Argument has an illustrious history dating back at least to the seventeenth century.[112] In broadest outline, the argument consists of these premises:

(1) Motivational internalism is true.
(2) The Humean theory of motivation is true.

We already saw motivational internalism in Section 4, and we saw the Humean theory earlier in this section. Depending on how they are formulated, motivational internalism and the Humean theory are thought to support the conclusion that:

---

[111] Another debate not discussed here has to with the nature of good moral reasons. For a helpful overview, see Tiberius 2015: chapter four.

[112] For discussion of the argument, see Smith 1994 and Shafer-Landau 2003b.

(3) Therefore moral cognitivism is false.

What is moral cognitivism? It is the leading position in meta-ethics on the psychology of moral judgments. We said in Section 1 that according to cognitivism, when I make a moral judgment such as "slavery is wrong," I am expressing my *belief* that slavery is wrong, as opposed to a desire in opposition to slavery. This seems to be the right thing to say about moral judgments. They do appear to have a cognitive or belief-like profile, rather than a noncognitive or desire-like profile. For instance, just as you would expect from a belief, our moral judgments seem to be true or false. If someone says that enslaving people in America was good, they are saying something false. Expressions of desires, on the other hand, are not capable of being true or false.

Why do motivational internalism and the Humean theory together lead us away from thinking of moral judgments as beliefs? Let's start again at the top of the Motivation Argument and write out the premises more explicitly:

(1*) Necessarily, if any person judges that some available action is morally right for her to perform or refrain from performing, then that person is motivated at least to some extent to perform or refrain from performing that action.
(2*) Necessarily, what motivates a person to act is a desire and not a belief.
(3*) Therefore moral judgments are not beliefs.

Put less formally, if only desires motivate, and a moral judgment has to motivate, then the moral judgment itself had better be a desire. If it were to be a belief instead, then there would be no guarantee that it would motivate the person to act.

If the Motivation Argument is sound, then cognitivism is false. That would have tremendous implications for meta-ethics. Most of the views that philosophers have defended are cognitivist views, and they would all go out the window.[113] To take one noteworthy example, we can add an additional premise as follows:

(4) Moral objectivism entails moral cognitivism.
(5) Therefore moral objectivism is false.

Moral objectivism, often labeled 'moral realism,' is the view that morality exists objectively and so independently of human invention or construction. It might have been created by a divine being, or it might just exist on its own, but an objective morality is one that we human beings did not play a role in bringing about. If there is an objective morality, then it is natural to think that our moral judgments would be true or false depending upon whether they

---

[113] For an overview of the positions in meta-ethics, see Miller 2011.

reflect that objective morality. But given (3) and the relationship between moral objectivism and moral cognitivism, we get (5).

So the Motivation Argument does some serious work. Indeed, according to the philosopher Michael Smith, how to think about motivational internalism, the Humean theory, and moral cognitivism together is *the* central problem in meta-ethics.[114] One way to undermine the argument is to reject motivational internalism, as I suggested in the previous section we should do. But given that there are restricted versions of motivational internalism that still might be plausible, it is worth seeing whether another way out of the argument is to reject the Humean theory of motivation.

5.3 Motivating the Humean Theory of Motivation

This is easier said than done. The Humean theory enjoys widespread support among philosophers – and for good reason. There are a number of reasonable arguments for the view. Here I briefly mention two of the leading ones.[115]

The Argument from Continuity. When we observe certain other animals in nature, it seems that they are motivated to perform various actions, and further-more that their motivation for action stems from desires they have – their instincts, impulses, wants, and the like.

Similarly in the human case, many infants seem motivated to behave in various ways by their basic wants and desires when, for example, they cry for food or need a diaper change. Even among adult humans, some actions seem to be the product of passing whims, brief impulses, or instinctive reactions. Surely we want to say that these actions are motivated actions, and here too the correct story about motivation seems to be the one told by the Humean.

The argument from continuity takes these observations and adds to them the premise that the story about motivation for adult humans who act for reasons ought to be continuous with the story about motivation for nonhuman animals, human infants, and adult humans who act on whims or impulses. Thus, on the grounds of continuity and uniformity, we ought to accept the Humean theory as the best theory about motivation in general.[116]

The Teleological Argument. The philosopher Michael Smith developed what has become perhaps the most discussed argument in recent philosophy which

---

[114] Smith 1994, a book which is entitled *The Moral Problem*.

[115] For a helpful survey of positive arguments for the Humean theory, see Shafer-Landau 2003b: 127–140. Shafer-Landau presents five different arguments, two of which are discussed in this subsection.

[116] My presentation of the argument from continuity follows Shafer-Landau 2003b: 131–132.

attempts to support some version of the Humean theory.[117] His teleological argument goes like this:

(a) Having a motivating reason is, *inter alia*, having a goal.[118]
(b) Having a goal is being in a state with which the world must fit.
(c) Being in a state with which the world must fit is desiring.[119]

Motivating reasons are just what motivate someone to act. From a more objective perspective, they may be good reasons or they may be bad reasons, but for the person in question they are playing a motivational role in her psychology.

That's pretty abstract, I know. To illustrate using our familiar example, we can say that Franklin has a motivating reason to visit Sally in the hospital. We can then run through Smith's argument as follows:

(a*) Having a motivating reason to visit Sally is, *inter alia*, having a goal to visit Sally.
(b*) Having a goal to visit Sally is being in a state with which the world must fit so that it becomes the case that Franklin visits Sally.
(c*) Being in a state with which the world must fit so that it becomes the case that Franklin visits Sally is Franklin's desiring that he visit Sally.

This looks like pretty smooth sailing so far.

But unlike the argument from continuity, here let me make a quick comment. It does seem right that at least one way in which Franklin can have this goal is for the following to be true of him:

> Franklin desires that he visit Sally.

But another way in which he might have this goal is with a belief:

> Franklin believes that it is morally valuable or required that he visit Sally.

It seems that he could take on the goal of visiting Sally if he forms such a belief. That belief might be inspired by thinking about the importance of his friendship with her and how lonely she must be in the hospital.

If this is right, then we need to recast Smith's argument as follows:

(a) Having a motivating reason is, *inter alia*, having a goal.
(b) Having a goal is either (i) being in a state with which the world must fit or (ii) being in a state with which the mind must fit and which concerns the moral importance of something that is not currently the case.

---

[117] For the original statement of the argument, see Smith 1987.

[118] '*inter alia*' means 'among other things.'

[119] This version appears in Smith 1994: 116. See also Smith 1987: 55.

(c) Being in a state with which the world must fit is desiring.

(d) Being in a state with which the mind must fit, and which concerns the moral importance of something that is not currently the case, is believing in a certain way.

(e) Therefore, having a motivating reason is, *inter alia*, either (i) desiring or (ii) believing in a certain way.

But if this is how the argument should go, then we no longer have an argument for the Humean theory. In fact, all we have is a choice between three options:

(1) Having a motivating reason is always, *inter alia*, desiring.

(2) Having a motivating reason is always, *inter alia*, believing in a certain way.

(3) Having a motivating reason is sometimes, *inter alia*, desiring and sometimes, *inter alia*, believing in a certain way.

But these are the very options which the whole debate is about in the first place. Hence, it may seem that the teleological argument by itself does not advance this debate.[120]

5.4 Doubts about the Humean and Anti-Humean Theories of Motivation

Not surprisingly, some of the controversy surrounding the Humean theory of motivation has centered around whether there are any plausible cases of beliefs which motivate action, and which thereby serve as compelling counterexamples to the Humean theory. Here is one example which has received a fair amount of attention, as stated by the philosopher Connie Rosati:

> Consider the individual who convinces herself that she has a desire she in fact lacks, such as the desire to become a lawyer. She enrolls in law school only to find herself unmotivated by her coursework, and drops out of school once a summer spent working as a carpenter reveals her love of carpentry. What most plausibly explains the individual's enrollment in law school and her

---

[120] Perhaps Michael Smith just intended the teleological argument to support what we have called the Desire Thesis – namely, that in order for a person to be motivated to perform a particular action, she must desire doing it. So then it would be no surprise that the teleological argument does not deliver as an argument for the *Humean theory* since, as we saw, the Humean also requires that the desire be the *source* of the motivation.

However, Smith is clear that he is a full-blown Humean about motivation, stating in a number of places that the mere presence of a desire is not enough for motivation and that motivation must have its source in the desire. The way he describes the teleological argument seems like he means it to support that view. See, for example, Smith 1994: 92–93, 125. Thanks to an anonymous reviewer for suggesting that I clarify this.

half-hearted efforts during that first year would seem to be her mistaken belief that she desired to become a lawyer.[121]

Given that she does not in fact desire to be a lawyer, it is hard to see how a desire would be what motivated her to enroll in law school. Humeans, in turn, have developed responses to this and other cases.[122]

In the remainder of this section, I want to briefly mention a more recent and bolder strategy which, if successfully employed, could cause trouble for both Humean and Anti-Humean theories of motivation all at once. I have developed this strategy at length elsewhere, as have others.[123]

One key move of this strategy is to support the following:

(FPP) From the first-person perspective, what motivates my actions are not my mental states but rather the contents of my mental states.

Let's unpack this terminology. By *mental states* I mean pairs of mental attitudes and contents such as my belief that p, your desire that q, and her wish that r. Believing, desiring, wishing, and the like are mental attitudes directed at mental contents, in this case p, q, and r. So, according to (FPP), what motivates us are not our beliefs, desires, wishes, or mental states more generally, but rather the *contents* of at least some of those mental states.

What are *mental contents*? Loosely speaking, they are that which people believe, desire, wish, and the like. This might sound as if contents are facts in the world. But we definitely do not want to say that, for we can be motivated by something that gets the facts all wrong. Hence, I might be motivated to drive to the party on Faculty Drive when in fact the party is on Student Drive.

So, by 'mental contents' I mean *mental representations of facts in the world*. If I believe there is widespread starvation in Iceland, what motivates me to donate to famine relief in Iceland can be the content of that belief – namely, *there is widespread starvation in Iceland*. This can happen even if the belief is *false* and there is in fact almost no starvation in Iceland.

Why should we accept (FPP), the claim that from our own internal perspective we are motivated by the contents of mental states? One source of evidence can be found in our ordinary explanations of our actions to others.[124] Thus, when asked why I performed a particular action rather than some other, my natural response might be:

---

[121] Rosati 2016, summarizing an example from Shafer-Landau 2003b: 125.

[122] See Rosati 2016 for a helpful overview.

[123] See Dancy 2000, Miller 2008b, and Turri 2009.   [124] See Darwall 1983: 31.

"I bought the second volume of her series because the first one was so good."
"I made the donation because people are starving in Africa and I can afford to
    help out."
"I jumped out of the way because the bicyclist was about to crash into me."
"I went to the hospital to see her because she is my friend."

Note the appeal only to our representations of facts in the world, and not to
anything about our psychological states themselves. In other words, the answers
that I offer to others typically are concerned with the quality of books, starvation
in various countries, immediate threats to my health, or my friend's well-being,
rather than what my beliefs and desires are.[125]

Thus far we have only been concerned with what motivates us from the *first*-
person perspective. What changes if we shift to a third-person perspective of
trying to explain what motivated *someone else* to act? My answer, in short, is:
not much. In a bit more detail, I say that:

(TPP) From the third-person perspective, what motivates a person to act is to be
    found in the contents of the same mental states that motivate the person to act
    from the first-person perspective.[126]

So, when I say that what motivated me to make the donation was the widespread
starvation in Iceland, so too should my wife (or my parents or friends or
a scientist overseeing a study) say that what motivated me to make the donation
was the widespread starvation in Iceland. It follows that what motivates in both
first- and third-person explanations is the same kind of thing. In fact, the matter
is even more straightforward since what motivates in both cases are precisely
the *very same things*, namely the same mental content.

Let us briefly consider the two main alternatives to (TPP), and why they are
not as plausible.

What Motivates are Facts in Third-Person Explanations. One alternative is to
say that facts in the world serve as what motivate people when we explain why
they behaved the way that they did. Thus, we might say that what explained why
a person jumped out of the road was the fact that the bus was about to hit him.

---

[125] Admittedly, we also say things like "I ran because I thought I was late" and "I went to the movie
    because I wanted to see something by that director." But these explanations need not conflict
    with (FPP). Of the following:
    My belief that *p*
    That I believe *p*
    the second is perfectly consistent with (FPP), since it is also the content of a mental state. For
    more, see Darwall 1983: 33, and Dancy 2000: chapter six.
[126] See also Darwall 1983: 29–33, and Scanlon 1998: chapter one.

Unfortunately, the same problem that arose for the first-person analog of this view also applies equally well when we shift to the third-person perspective. In many cases we are *mistaken* about what the relevant facts really are, and so it will be of little help to appeal to those facts in an explanation for why someone acted as he did. For instance, it does not help to explain my behavior to mention that the liquid was really contaminated when I thought it was regular water. If I had known it was contaminated, I never would have tasted it in the first place. But given my ignorance, the fact that the water was contaminated doesn't help at all to explain what I did.

What Motivates are Mental States in Third-Person Explanations. Here we return to the familiar ground occupied by Humean and Anti-Humean theories of motivation. When we explain what motivated someone's action, we should appeal to their mental states.[127]

What motivated me to drink the water? A Humean might say that it was my *desire* to drink the water so as to not be thirsty any more. An Anti-Humean might say the same thing, or instead focus on a *belief* that the water would be a good means for relieving my thirst. Either way, these explanations of my behavior center on my mental states: my beliefs and desires.

But there are two problems with this.[128] First of all, we already said that from the first-person perspective, mental states are not what motivate action. The contents of those states do. From my own perspective, I was motivated by how the water would quench my thirst. Now, though, from the third-person perspective we are saying that mental states are what motivate – that is, my beliefs or desires. But that might seem absurd. How can a successful third-person explanation of motivation appeal to something which the person doesn't regard as motivating him?

Turn now to the second problem. It tries to reduce the mental state approach to absurdity by focusing on *good* reasons. Good reasons are plausibly understood as facts. To see this, return to our familiar example of Sally in the hospital. Franklin is considering whether to visit Sally, and decides to go because she is his friend and she is lonely. Suppose, as seems highly plausible, that this is a good reason for visiting Sally. A good reason like this is a *fact*: it is a fact that she is his friend and she is lonely. Franklin is able to grasp that fact psychologically. It is the content of one of his mental states. But it is not a mental state itself. The good reason is not a belief, for instance, but could be the content of a belief.

Here's the problem. If we explain Franklin's behavior by appealing to his mental states of belief and desire, as both Humeans and Anti-Humeans do, it would follow that human beings never, strictly speaking, act for good reasons. Those reasons are

---

[127] Many sources could be cited here. For a few examples, see Smith 1987, 1994: chapter four, and Cuneo 2002: 466–467.

[128] For more extensive discussion, see Dancy 2000 and Miller 2008b.

not mental states like beliefs and desires; they are simply of a different kind from the mental states which are supposed to be what motivate action.

Leaving these other problematic views aside, then, I think we should accept the proposal in (TPP). In other words, when we explain what motivates someone else to act, we should appeal to the *contents* of their mental states. Then the problems go away. What motivates in both first- and third-person explanations is the same (e.g., what Franklin believes, namely that Sally is his friend and she is lonely), and what motivates can be a good reason for action (e.g., the fact that Sally is his friend and she is lonely, which is represented in the content of his belief).

Such an approach provides a simple and elegant story about our motivational lives. If we accept it, though, we will have to abandon both the Humean and Anti-Humean theories of motivation.

6 Conscious Moral Reasoning and Our Feelings: Three Views about the Psychology of Moral Judgments

One of the liveliest areas in moral psychology in recent years has been research on the extent to which conscious reasoning leads to the formation of moral judgments. The goal of this final section is to review and briefly assess three of the leading positions on this topic.[129]

Two quick comments before we begin. First, the primary focus of this discussion is on *descriptive* issues about how people actually form their moral judgments. Hence, we will not say much about normative questions concerning the ways people *should* go about forming them. Second, and closely related, the main source of descriptive data in this discussion is research in psychology. This includes neuroscientific and behavioral experiments.

We will begin with some background on what the central issues are and how the terminology is to be understood. Then we will take up each of the three positions: traditional rationalism, social intuitionism, and modern rationalism.

6.1. Background

Let's return to Sally and Franklin. Here is the case again:

> *The Hospital Visit.* Sally breaks her leg in a skiing accident. She has been in the hospital for several days without any visitors, so she texts her friend Franklin, tells him what happened, and mentions the name of the hospital in the hope that he will come to visit her.
> When Franklin reads Sally's text, he decides that he should go visit Sally in the hospital that afternoon. A few hours later, he walks into her hospital

---

[129] This section is adapted from Miller 2019b, with permission of Routledge.

Figure 3 Three Stages Pertaining to Franklin's Judgment about Visiting Sally

room. Sally is very glad to see him, and they have a very enjoyable time together.

Franklin's moral judgment is that he should visit Sally in the hospital that afternoon. From the story, we do not know what considerations led him to form that judgment. We also do not know the extent to which his judgment was formed on the basis of conscious as opposed to unconscious deliberation. Finally, let me now add that when Sally sees him, she asks Franklin why he decided to come see her. He replies, "Because you are my friend and I care about you." But we also do not know whether this is an accurate representation of what led to his judgment, even if Franklin is being sincere in his statement.

Figure 3 illustrates how we might break down what was going on with Franklin's judgment into three stages. Let me briefly comment on each of these stages.

Stage One. Our main question pertaining to Stage One is going to be the following:

Question 1: Is conscious moral reasoning typically involved in the formation of a moral judgment?

Note that the question is about what 'typically' happens. Few would deny that there are cases where moral judgments are formed spontaneously without any prior conscious reasoning. The debate, as we will see, is about whether this is the typical way that moral judgments are formed, or whether it is the exception.

'Moral reasoning' can be understood very broadly here as involving a process of weighing considerations prior to a decision about what to think or what to do. An example would be evaluating arguments on both sides of the death penalty debate before coming to a conclusion about whether it is morally wrong for a particular person to be executed. Of course, other cases of reasoning need not involve this much abstract reflection. They could be a matter of, say, thinking about what Jesus or Gandhi would do, or what your mother always told you to do, and then, on the basis of that answer, coming to form a moral judgment.

Two other closely related questions are typically brought up in this literature. The first one is the following:

Question 2: Are moral principles typically involved in the formation of a moral judgment?

'Moral principles' can also be understood broadly here, as principles connecting some nonmoral facts with some moral evaluation such as goodness, rightness, or virtue.[130] Examples of principles people might hold include:

Abortion is wrong.
If it would cause people a lot of pain, then don't do it.
If children in Africa could use the supplies, then we shouldn't waste them.
I morally have to keep my promises.

Back to Question 2. It is asking whether we typically form moral judgments on the basis of one or more moral principles, regardless of how plausible or sophisticated or even coherent those principles might be. For instance, when I judged that I should keep my promise to Samantha, did I form the judgment using a more general principle about keeping promises, such as "I morally have to keep my promises"? Again, these are empirical issues, which are distinct from a normative discussion of the plausibility of the principles themselves. The question is about whether we actually use moral principles in making moral judgments, not whether the principles are true or false.

The third question is this one:

Question 3: Are moral judgments typically formed on the basis of moral reasons?

Moral reasons are morally relevant considerations which count in favor of (or against) a particular action. Specifically, the reasons here are subjective or motivating reasons; they are good moral reasons from the person's own perspective.[131] But they need not really be good moral reasons.

Back to our example: suppose Franklin formed his judgment about the rightness of visiting Sally on the basis of it being the loving thing to do. Then, his judgment would clearly be based on a moral reason, and in this case it is a good moral reason too. Suppose instead, though, that he formed the judgment because he didn't want Sally to call him a bad friend behind his back if he didn't visit. In this version, Franklin would not have a good reason for forming his moral judgment, even if he thinks that he does. The judgment would be based on reasons which motivate him, but which are not good reasons.

---

[130] For relevant discussion, see Horgan and Timmons 2007: 283.

[131] Motivating reasons were discussed in the previous section as well, in connection to Michael Smith's argument for the Humean theory of motivation.

Now, it might seem overly much to distinguish between these three questions. After all, if we answer any one of them affirmatively, wouldn't we have to do the same for the other two? But this is not something we should simply assume from the start. In fact, as we will see, the position called 'modern rationalism' can only exist as an intelligible view if the answers to these three questions come apart.

Stage Two. We can be neutral on the nature of moral judgments, and in particular whether cognitivism or noncognitivism is correct. For our purposes we can simply understand moral judgments as the person's conclusion about the moral status of something. The moral status could involve axiology (goodness, badness, etc.), deontology (rightness, wrongness, obligatory, etc.), or character (virtuous, honest, cruel, etc.). The object of a judgment could range over people ("Stalin was cruel"), actions ("What John Smith did was morally wrong"), and outcomes ("The consequences of her decision were awful"), among other things.

Stage Three. When Sally asked Franklin why he thought he should come visit her, he replied, "Because you are my friend and I care about you." Suppose he was not trying to deceive her, and he really did take this to be the reason why he formed his judgment. But was it the reason, after all? In other words, the fourth and final question that is central in this discussion is the following:

Question 4: When people give sincere explanations for why they formed their moral judgments, are those explanations typically accurate?

The 'sincere' is important, since obviously if a person is out to deceive others about these matters, then the resulting 'explanation' will not typically be accurate.

Franklin's answer is sincere, and that could have been what led him to form his judgment about visiting Sally. But it might not have been. It might have been something rather different, such as not wanting to be the subject of negative gossip, a feeling which he did not realize was actually at work in Stage One. As a result, if it was this feeling that was responsible for his judgment, then Franklin is guilty of what's called *post-hoc confabulation*. He made up a story, perhaps without even realizing that this was what he was doing. Even though the story had little basis in reality, he believed it to be true.

As we will see, there is sharp disagreement among researchers working in this area about the prevalence of post-hoc confabulation in our moral psychology. But enough background for now. Let's get to the views themselves.

6.2 Traditional Rationalism

With the demise of behaviorism in psychology, a rationalist approach to the psychology of moral judgments became prominent in the 1960s and '70s. Concerning Stage One, traditional rationalism offers a unified answer to all three questions:

> Typically moral judgments are formed on the basis of conscious moral reasoning, they are formed on the basis of one or more moral principles, and they are formed on the basis of one or more moral reasons.

In other words, the answer is 'yes' to all three questions.

What about after the moral judgment is formed in Stage Three? Here, traditional rationalists answer 'yes' to the fourth question as well. When people give sincere explanations for why they formed their moral judgments, those explanations typically are accurate.

So, in our example it is likely that "Because you are my friend and I care about you" really was why Franklin thought visiting Sally was right. If Franklin's is a typical case, then according to traditional rationalism his friendship with Sally was something he consciously considered when evaluating his behavior, even if it was just a quick thought. His friendship was the primary reason for his judgment, and he might have used a principle such as "If someone is my friend then I should help them when they are in need of help." Principle, reason, conscious reasoning, and accurate explanation.

The figure most often associated with traditional rationalism is the psychologist Lawrence Kohlberg. The details of his well-known six-stage view need not concern us here. At the general level, though, Kohlberg wrote that the "stages were defined in terms of free responses to ten hypothetical moral dilemmas,"[132] indicating his trust in the general accuracy of the justifications people offered for their moral judgments. Furthermore, according to Kohlberg those judgments are typically the product of moral principles: "it is no more surprising to find that cognitive moral principles determine choice of conflicting social actions than it is to find that cognitive scientific principles determine choice of conflicting actions on physical objects."[133]

Traditional rationalism has a lot going for it. It preserves widely held views about the central role of reasoning, reasons, and principles in moral agency. It avoids skeptical conclusions about the justification for our moral judgments and our first-person explanations for them. In denying the pervasiveness of post-hoc confabulation, it also resonates well with our experience of offering accounts of why we judge things the way we do, morally speaking. After all, it does not

---

[132] Kohlberg 1969: 375.   [133] Ibid., 397.

seem to us that we are making up a story to fit our judgment, but rather that we are telling a true story about what preceded that judgment.

Despite these advantages, today traditional rationalism is almost universally rejected by psychologists and philosophers alike.[134] Here are three commonly raised problems for the view, the first two of which apply to traditional rationalism's account of Stage One and the last to its account of Stage Three:

First Objection: Bad Fit with Our Experience. Traditional rationalism does a poor job of capturing our experience at Stage One. Much of the time, we do not undergo conscious deliberation, reflection, or the like prior to forming a moral judgment. Rather, we experience the judgment as immediately arising within us. This is true most obviously when we have little time to act. But it is true in more mundane cases as well, such as the Franklin and Sally example. Franklin got the text from Sally. He concluded that he should visit her. No conscious reasoning seemed to be involved in the middle.

Second Objection: Bad Fit with the Neuroscientific Evidence. Psychologists Antonio Damasio and Joshua Greene, among others, have conducted studies of the neuroscience of moral judgment formation which are frequently taken to show the central role of emotional responses. One implication of their work is meant to be that "When emotion is removed from decision making, people do not become hyperlogical and hyperethical; they become unable to feel the rightness and wrongness of simple decisions and judgments."[135] This is supposed to be trouble for traditional rationalism since traditional rationalism downplays the role of emotion by focusing on conscious reasoning and moral principles.[136]

Third Objection: Bad Fit with the Confabulation Evidence. Recall that Stage Three concerns explaining why we formed a moral judgment after we have already done so. According to traditional rationalism, at Stage Three a person's explanation for his own moral judgments will typically be accurate.

But in a series of well-known studies, psychologist Jonathan Haidt found that participants struggled mightily when presented with various scenarios and asked to justify their moral judgments about them. Here is the best known of his cases:

> Julie and Mark are brother and sister. They are traveling together in France on summer vacation from college. One night they are staying alone in a cabin

---

[134] For critical discussion, see Haidt 2001 and Haidt and Bjorklund 2008a.

[135] Haidt and Bjorklund 2008a: 198.

[136] For more, see Damasio 1994; Haidt 2001: 823–825, Greene and Haidt 2002, and Haidt and Bjorklund 2008a: 199–201.

near the beach. They decide that it would be interesting and fun if they tried making love. At the very least it would be a new experience for each of them. Julie was already taking birth control bills, but Mark uses a condom too, just to be safe. They both enjoy making love, but they decide not to do it again. They keep that night as a special secret, which makes them feel even closer to each other. What do you think about that? Was it OK for them to make love?[137]

As Haidt and Fredrik Bjorklund summarize the findings of this research, "Very quick judgment was followed by a search for supporting reasons only; when these reasons were stripped away by the experimenter, few subjects changed their minds, even though many confessed that they could not explain the reasons for their decisions."[138]

In the example above, participants judge that Julie and Mark making love was wrong, but it is not clear that they had any principled or reasons-based justification for saying this. All the usual reasons – it could lead to a child with genetic abnormalities, it could damage their relationship in the future, and so forth – don't apply in this particular story. Rather, it can seem as if participants form the judgment on some nonrational basis, and then afterwards try to invent a story to justify why they made the judgment in the first place. This is post-hoc confabulation, and it is incompatible with traditional rationalism's account of Stage Three reasoning.

These problems, among others, inspired a search for another approach to understanding the psychology of moral judgments. Eventually, social intuitionism emerged as a popular alternative.

6.3 Social Intuitionism

Given the problems confronting traditional rationalism, and given developments in other areas of psychology at the time, the stage was set in the 1990s for the emergence of what came to be called *social intuitionism*. Haidt himself was the leading exponent of the view, and it received its famous statement in his 2001 paper, "The Emotional Dog and Its Rational Tail: A Social Intuitionist Approach to Moral Judgment."[139]

Our first question was about whether conscious moral reasoning is typically involved in the formation of moral judgments. Social intuitionism has a clear answer: 'no.'[140] Whatever is involved in typical cases, it will be doing its work

---

[137] Haidt 2001: 814.   [138] Haidt and Bjorklund 2008a: 198.

[139] Haidt 2001. See also Greene and Haidt 2002, Haidt 2003, Haidt and Joseph 2004, and Haidt and Bjorklund 2008a, 2008b. For work in philosophy that overlaps in various ways with social intuitionism, see Nichols 2004 and Prinz 2007.

[140] Haidt 2001: 818–820, and Haidt and Bjorklund 2008a: 189.

subconsciously. To clarify a bit more, Haidt and Bjorklund describe a *conscious* process as being "intentional, effortful, and controllable and that the reasoner is aware that it is going on," and *reasoning* as having "steps, at least two of which are performed consciously."[141] The formation of a moral judgment does not involve conscious reasoning, at least standardly.

What does cause moral judgments, then? Haidt and his colleagues are clear here too: moral judgments are typically caused by moral intuitions,[142] defined as:

> the sudden appearance in consciousness, or at the fringe of consciousness, of an evaluative feeling about the character or actions of a person, without any conscious awareness of having gone through steps of searching, weighing evidence, or inferring a conclusion.[143]

To return to our example, Franklin's judgment could have been caused by a moral intuition prompted by thoughts of Sally's injury, an intuition which spontaneously and subconsciously brought about the moral judgment. Such a process of going from intuition to judgment, at any rate, is supposed to be the typical causal pathway according to social intuitionism.

How about our second question concerning whether *moral principles* are typically involved in Stage One, the stage having to do with what leads to the formation of a moral judgment? Here, social intuitionism is clear again: 'no, they are not typically involved.' Indeed, Franklin might accept some moral principles about what it takes to be a good friend, and they even could have produced exactly the same judgment in favor of visiting Sally in the hospital *if* they had been used. But according to social intuitionism, such principles will normally be bypassed or ignored. Instead our intuitions do the work, and in this example they lead Franklin straight to the judgment about visiting Sally.

The third question concerns the contribution of *moral reasons*. Here it is a bit less clear what social intuitionism has to say, as I am not aware of any passages in which Haidt and company address this issue directly. But a natural reading of their work suggests that the answer will be 'no' as well. Suppose we assume that forming moral judgments on the basis of moral reasons requires *conscious* reasoning. Add to that the claim that conscious reasoning is rare prior to judgment formation. It then follows that moral judgments will rarely be formed on the basis of moral reasons.

To summarize the picture of Stage One according to social intuitionism, people typically form moral judgments on the basis of moral intuitions, and

---

[141] Haidt and Bjorklund 2008a: 189.
[142] Haidt 2001: 817, and Haidt and Bjorklund 2008a: 188.
[143] Haidt and Bjorklund 2008a: 188.

not on the basis of conscious reasoning, principles, or reasons. Hence, we have a view which is diametrically opposed to traditional rationalism.

That opposition extends to Stage Three, where the question is about the accuracy of our sincere attempts to explain our own moral judgments. Social intuitionism is happy to admit that people at Stage Three often *do* engage in conscious moral reasoning.[144] Unfortunately, though, according to social intuitionism what they come up with in explaining their particular moral judgments is usually not accurate. In particular, social intuitionism endorses the following:

> *Postjudgment Confabulation*: The appeals to various reasons and principles after the formation of a moral judgment are typically confabulatory on the part of the individual since there were in fact no causally influential reasons and principles in the first place.

Hence, Haidt and Bjorklund write that "moral reasoning is an effortful process (as opposed to an automatic process) usually engaged in after a moral judgment is made, in which a person searches for arguments that will support an already-made judgment."[145]

Sally asks Franklin why he decided to come visit her. At this point, he consciously reflects for a minute, then replies "Because you are my friend and I care about you. It's what friends do for each other." He is invoking a moral principle about friendship, and suggesting that it was what led him to form his moral judgment about visiting Sally, back when he was still at home. But social intuitionists will suggest that Franklin is likely confabulating. He is inventing this story now, in the hospital, but it does not reflect what actually prompted Franklin's judgment, which was instead a subconscious feeling. Hence, Franklin is guilty of postjudgment confabulation.

The above captures the heart of social intuitionism as I understand the view.[146] There is also much to be said in favor of this position, as there was for traditional rationalism. To begin, it avoids the three problems that were raised for traditional rationalism. Thus, social intuitionism claims to capture our experience of immediately forming moral judgments in many cases without going through any prior conscious reasoning. The second problem raised for rationalism was that it supposedly fit badly with the neuroscientific evidence. That evidence was said to support the centrality of emotions to the process of

---

[144] Ibid., 189.

[145] Ibid. See also Haidt 2001: 814, 817, 820–823, and Haidt and Bjorklund 2008a:189, 2008b: 249.

[146] Haidt has also tried to categorize the intuitions people typically have into five sets of basic intuitions: harm/care, fairness/reciprocity, authority/respect, purity/sanctity, and in-group/out-group. He has even offered an evolutionary account for why those particular kinds of intuitions would have likely emerged over time (Haidt and Joseph 2004 and Haidt and Bjorklund 2008a: 203–204).

forming moral judgments, and it fits well with the emphasis of social intuitionism on the role of moral intuitions. Finally, the pervasiveness of "making things up" about why we form the moral judgments that we do is a central commitment of social intuitionism and its emphasis on the role of post-hoc confabulation.[147]

However, social intuitionism has had no shortage of critics. Here, I highlight only two of the more serious objections that have arisen. They both pertain to social intuitionism's account of Stage One.[148]

First Objection: Overreaching.[149] As Haidt initially formulated social intuitionism, it appears to apply to all of the moral judgments a person makes. But if so, then according to the objection, social intuitionism badly overreaches. This point has been made most forcefully by the psychologist Darcia Narvaez.[150] She calls attention to the important role of other factors at Stage One besides intuitions, such as the person's goals and values as well as the frequency of conscious reasoning. To take an example, as I drive home I might see a homeless person asking for money at the street corner, and ask myself what I should do. No answer immediately comes to mind. I might reflect on how a few dollars could help him avoid being hungry tonight. But then I remember that there are plenty of shelters in this area offering free food and a clean bed. Perhaps I could have a bigger impact by putting the money to work with a famine relief organization in Africa. Eventually, though, I come to decide that the right thing to do is to help the homeless person out. Intuitions, goals, values, and conscious deliberation all seemed to play a role in arriving at this judgment. As Narvaez writes, often "[i]nstead of intuition's dominating the process, intuition danced with conscious reasoning, taking turns doing the leading."[151]

In their response to Narvaez, Haidt and Bjorklund make a surprising concession. They in effect revise social intuitionism so that it pertains to a much narrower class of moral judgments – namely, moral judgments a person makes *about someone else* (her character, her actions, and the like). With respect to first-person moral judgments, or judgments about my own character, actions, and the like, Haidt and Bjorklund concede Narvaez's objection and acknowledge that social intuitionism is not a plausible view for such cases.[152]

This is a major concession. So many of the moral judgments we make are about ourselves. Should I give money to the homeless person? Is it important to

---

[147] For more on this and other evidence offered in favor of social intuitionism, see Haidt 2001: 819–825, Greene and Haidt 2002, and Haidt and Bjorklund 2008a: 196–201.

[148] For additional critical discussion of social intuitionism, see Pizarro and Bloom 2003, Sneddon 2007, Jacobson 2008, Sauer 2011, and Railton 2014.

[149] The presentation of this objection draws on an expanded discussion in Miller 2016: 33–35.

[150] Narvaez 2008.   [151] Ibid., 235.   [152] Haidt and Bjorklund 2008b: 242–244, 249.

keep my promise? Would it really be so bad for me to bend the truth a little bit? Thus, social intuitionism becomes narrower in scope by not pertaining to those judgments. And now we also need to find another account of the psychology of our first-person moral judgments.

But matters are worse than this. For the first-person versus third-person distinction does not do the work that Haidt and Bjorklund need it to do. On the one hand, there are many cases of first-person moral judgments which do *not* involve conscious reasoning, and which seem to fit well with the social intuitionism account. Haidt and Bjorklund themselves even offer an example of someone spontaneously deciding to jump into a river to save a drowning person.[153] But consider, on the other hand, that there are many cases of third-person moral judgments which *do* involve conscious reasoning, including the "private, internal, conscious weighing of options and consequences."[154] Someone deliberating about the morality of the death penalty, or more specifically about the morality of a particular judge ordering the death penalty for a convicted murderer, serves as a clear example.[155]

At this point Haidt and Bjorklund might be wise to just abandon the first-person/third-person distinction and acknowledge that the story about our Stage One moral psychology is messier than they had first envisioned. Moral intuitions play a role, but so do goals, principles, values, conscious reasoning, and the like. The extent to which each of them does so will vary from person to person and situation to situation.

Second Objection: Results from Affect Psychology. In recent decades in psychology, an emerging picture paints emotions and feelings as much more sophisticated information-processing systems than does the picture that emerges from social intuitionism of "quick gut-feelings,"[156] which are nonrational and so not sensitive to reasons and values. The philosopher Peter Railton has provided a helpful review of this literature and its implications for social intuitionism. As he notes, there is now support for the idea that emotions "could actually constitute appropriate representations of value ... an element of practical knowledge that could guide action 'in the right way' to make it responsive to reasons ... [W]ell-attuned [emotions] can be fitting responses to value."[157] For instance, subconsciously our empathetic emotions can help us to grasp the feelings of others around us and come to feel what they are feeling. These responses can provide us with a source for good reasons to make a moral judgment. After empathetically becoming aware of my friend's suffering and feeling something of what it is like

---

[153] Ibid., 244.   [154] Ibid., 242.

[155] For further development of this objection, see Miller 2016: 33–35.

[156] Haidt and Joseph 2004: 57. See also Haidt 2001: 817.   [157] Railton 2014: 840–841.

myself, I can conclude that I should drop what I am doing and try to help. This judgment is rational, and afterwards my explanation for why I made it – because my friend was suffering and needed my help – can be accurate.[158]

This contemporary research on emotions and feelings has the potential to challenge not only social intuitionism's response to the third question about reasons and moral judgments, but also their claim about the extent to which we are guilty of post-hoc confabulation.[159]

These are both serious problems for social intuitionism. And combined with the difficulties we saw earlier for traditional rationalism, it might be welcome news if a plausible third option emerges. Modern rationalism tries to be that option.

6.4 Modern Rationalism

Is there even any room for a third option? Initially it might seem that traditional rationalism and social intuitionism are not just mutually exclusive but are also the only options available. However, by carefully distinguishing between the different questions that might arise at Stage One, we can see a third way forward, which we might call 'modern rationalism.'[160] Several writers have developed positions in this area, and here I will focus specifically on the work of the philosophers Terry Horgan and Mark Timmons.[161] Let us spell out the details of their view by taking each of our four questions in turn.

For the first question about the extent of conscious reasoning, modern rationalism sides with social intuitionism in accepting that typically we form moral judgments spontaneously on the basis of subconscious processing. But, strikingly, it sides with traditional rationalism on the second and third questions. In other words, modern rationalism maintains that in typical cases, our moral judgments are formed on the basis of one or more moral principles that we accept, and they are formed for moral reasons. These are claims we saw that social intuitionism, at least as formulated above, cannot accept.[162]

How is modern rationalism able to deny a role for conscious reasoning in typical cases, while also affirming a role for moral principles and moral reasons? This combination can work, Horgan and Timmons claim, provided that principles and reasons are able to influence our thinking subconsciously. This is a possibility that Haidt and company seem to have overlooked, or at least

---

[158] Ibid., 842–843.   [159] For confabulation in particular, see ibid., 847–850.

[160] I am grateful to an anonymous reviewer for suggesting this label.

[161] Horgan and Timmons developed their position, which they call "morphological rationalism," first in a 2007 paper and more recently in a forthcoming book. In the text I will use the more general label 'modern rationalism.' For others who can be associated with this position, see Mikhail 2011, Railton 2014, and May 2018.

[162] See Horgan and Timmons 2007.

did not address in detail.[163] As Horgan and Timmons note, social intuitionists seem to just assume the following:

> *Assumption*: "Unless conscious moral reasoning is part of the process leading to moral judgment, subjects' reason-giving efforts are not a matter of citing considerations that really did play a causal role in the generation of the judgments in question; rather, reason-giving in these cases is a matter of confabulation."[164]

But Horgan and Timmons argue that this assumption is false. Even though we might experience our moral judgments as typically formed immediately and spontaneously, the underlying psychological processes could be highly complex and involve both principles and reasons. Hence, Horgan and Timmons answer no to the first question, and yes to the second and third questions. Thus, they claim, they can preserve the most plausible features of both traditional rationalism and social intuitionism.

So far we have focused on Stage One. What does modern rationalism have to say about Stage Three? Here it sides again with traditional rationalism. Horgan and Timmons acknowledge that in some cases we surely do engage in post-hoc confabulation by making up a story about why we formed the moral judgment that we did. But they consider these cases to be the exception rather than the rule. One of their main reasons for this is what they call the "non-jarringness of reason-giving experience," where "in sincerely giving reasons for one's … moral judgments, one typically experiences the giving of reasons as fitting smoothly with the experiences in which those judgments were formed, and as helping to make sense of those experiences."[165] When Franklin appealed to his friendship with Sally in explaining why he decided to visit her, this felt to him as fitting smoothly with his experience of forming the judgment in the first place. It felt like a completely natural thing for him to say, rather than being forced or awkward. Experiences like Franklin's of this smooth and natural fit need to be explained. Horgan and Timmons claim that there is a better explanation available than just appealing to massive confabulation as social intuitionism insists we do, namely to hold that people typically are being *accurate* in their post-judgment explanations, rather than making up a story to suit their judgments.[166]

Like traditional rationalism, modern rationalism has the advantage of fitting smoothly with our moral experience at Stage Three. But unlike traditional rationalism, it also has the advantage of capturing the experience of forming moral judgments spontaneously without prior conscious reasoning. In addition,

---

[163] The closest Haidt comes to discussing a view like modern rationalism, as far as I can tell, is in Haidt and Bjorklund 2008a: 212–213.

[164] Horgan and Timmons 2007: 282.   [165] Ibid., 291.   [166] Ibid., 293–294.

it can accept the important role of emotion in moral judgment formation. Indeed, given the recent research in psychology that was briefly mentioned earlier,[167] subconscious emotional states may even be one of the main sources of moral reasons for those judgments. Or, at the very least, they can come alongside moral principles and reasons in giving rise to judgments. So, as Horgan and Timmons see things, modern rationalism can deliver the best of traditional rationalism and social intuitionism, while at the same time avoiding their main difficulties.

Unfortunately, there has not been a great deal of work evaluating the view at this point in time.[168] So, while other objections will surely be raised once their book appears, let me raise a preliminary concern here for Horgan and Timmons, a concern which should also apply to other modern rationalists as well.[169] It has to do with the threat of skepticism.

Franklin spontaneously judges that he should visit Sally, and after the fact, when he is with Sally, he reports that he made the judgment because she is his friend. Now, leave aside for the moment whether this *really was* the basis for his moral judgment, and let's ask this question. When he is with Sally in the hospital and consciously reflects on his judgment to visit her (Stage Three), how is Franklin supposed to figure out why he earlier made the judgment to visit? There might have been many different reasons why he chose to do so. One possibility involves reasons of friendship. Another one, though, involves avoiding negative gossip. Yet another possibility involves avoiding feeling guilty if he does not visit. Still other possibilities are imaginable. Of course, one can always choose the most morally admirable one from the list, but its being admirable does not guarantee that it is the most plausible story about one's own mind.

The concern for modern rationalism lurking in this neighborhood is a form of skepticism:

> *Skepticism about our Reasons for Forming Moral Judgments*: Given the subconscious causal role of moral principles and reasons in leading to the formation of moral judgments, in any given instance where a moral judgment is formed spontaneously and immediately without conscious deliberation, the person in question has no reasonable basis upon which to discern what her actual reasons were for forming the judgment.[170]

---

[167] Railton 2014. [168] See Miller 2016.

[169] The concern draws from Miller 2016, with permission of Taylor and Francis. Future work can explore whether the concern also applies to the views developed by Mikhail 2011 and May 2018, which were cited earlier.

[170] See Miller 2016: 41.

To take a different example involving my own behavior instead of Franklin's, suppose I agree to help a stranger carry a heavy box of books. If we adopt modern rationalism, then I will not have enough to go on to decide whether my helping judgment arose from a subconsciously functioning moral principle, a subconscious desire to alleviate recent feelings of guilt or embarrassment, a subconscious desire to make the other person indebted to me, or a variety of other possibilities. I am left without a clear way to decide between them.

Again, none of this is meant to call into question the story modern rationalism has told about Stage One. There could be plenty of cases where our moral principles do generate a moral judgment in the way modern rationalism has suggested. The concern is not with Stage One but with Stage Three. If I say that I thought it was a good idea to help carry the boxes because I saw someone in serious need of help and it is a good thing to help people in serious need, then that might indeed have been what my subconscious thinking was like. But even so, I would only have gotten these facts correct *by accident*. I was not reliable about these matters. Therefore, in other situations I might invoke the same story, but instead guilt relief was really involved, and I messed up because I could not discern this from the first-person perspective.

The practical lesson becomes that, until I can devise a better way of figuring it out, I should avoid offering any explanation for how my moral judgments came about. Presumably I am not unique here. Most of us will be in a similar position, and so this is the skeptical worry about Stage Three.

Much more work would need to be done to develop this concern in detail, and no doubt Horgan and Timmons will have plenty to say in reply as they continue to develop the details of modern rationalism.

6.5 Conclusion

We have seen three of the leading positions on the psychology of moral judgments. Research in this area is still in its infancy, and there are exciting opportunities for philosophers and psychologists to work together to better understand how our minds typically work when it comes to forming moral judgments.

Indeed, the same could be said about all the issues we have discussed in this Element. The interdisciplinary field of moral psychology is just getting going.

Nevertheless, I want to suggest that some views look to be more plausible at this point in time than others. Franklin and Sally can help us one last time to sum up what they are:

> Franklin does not have to be visiting Sally for self-interested motives. He is capable of genuinely altruistic and dutiful motives too. Psychological egoism is false.

Virtues make up a good character, but if Franklin is like most people, his character falls short of being virtuous. Widespread possession of the virtues is implausible.

Franklin judged that he should visit Sally, and he was motivated accordingly. But he didn't have to be. He can make a moral judgment and not be motivated without being abnormal or practically irrational. Most versions of motivational internalism are false.

Franklin was motivated to visit Sally, but not by a desire and not by a belief. Rather, he was motivated by considerations in his mind, such as how good it would be to see her and how bad it would be for her to be lonely. Both the Humean and Anti-Humean theories of motivation are false.

When Franklin judged that he should visit Sally, he didn't go through a process of conscious deliberation. It was a decision he arrived at spontaneously and naturally, but at the same time it was a rational decision formed on the basis of reasons influencing him subconsciously. Modern rationalism is more plausible than traditional rationalism and social intuitionism.

Of course none of these claims is meant to be specific to Franklin. Our minds work much the same way when we are confronted with morally relevant situations too.

References

Alfano, Mark. (2013). *Character as Moral Fiction*. Cambridge: Cambridge University Press.

Baron, R. (1997). "The Sweet Smell of. . . Helping: Effects of Pleasant Ambient Fragrance on Prosocial Behavior in Shopping Malls." *Personality and Social Psychology Bulletin* 23: 498–503.

Bates, Tom and Pauline Kleingeld. (2018). "Virtue, Vice, and Situationism," in *The Oxford Handbook of Virtue*. Ed. Nancy E. Snow. New York: Oxford University Press, 524–545.

Batson, C., J. Dyck, J. Brandt, et al. (1988). "Five Studies Testing Two New Egoistic Alternatives to the Empathy-Altruism Hypothesis." *Journal of Personality and Social Psychology* 55: 52–77.

Batson, C., S. Early, and G. Salvarani. (1997). "Perspective Taking: Imagining How Another Feels Versus Imagining How You Would Feel." *Personality and Social Psychology Bulletin* 23: 751–758.

Batson, C. and J. Weeks. (1996). "Mood Effects of Unsuccessful Helping: Another Test of the Empathy-Altruism Hypothesis." *Personality and Social Psychology Bulletin* 22: 148–157.

Batson, D. (1991). *The Altruism Question: Toward a Social-Psychological Answer*. Hillsdale: Erlbaum.

(2002). "Addressing the Altruism Question Experimentally," in *Altruism and Altruistic Love: Science, Philosophy, and Religion in Dialogue*. Ed. S. Post, L. Underwood, J. Schloss, and W. Hurlbut. Oxford: Oxford University Press, 89–105.

(2011). *Altruism in Humans*. New York: Oxford University Press.

Battaly, Heather. (2015). *Virtue*. Cambridge: Polity Press.

Camerer, C. (2003). *Behavioral Game Theory: Experiments in Strategic Interaction*. Princeton: Princeton University Press.

Collins, John. (1988). "Belief, Desire, and Revision." *Mind* 97: 333–342.

Cuneo, Terence. (2002). "Reconciling Realism with Humeanism." *Australasian Journal of Philosophy* 80: 465–486.

Curzer, H. (2012). *Aristotle and the Virtues*. Oxford: Oxford University Press.

Damasio, A. (1994). *Descartes' Error: Emotion, Reason, and the Human Brain*. New York: Putnam.

Dana, J., D. Cain, and R. Dawes. (2006). "What You Don't Know Won't Hurt Me: Costly (but Quiet) Exit in Dictator Games." *Organizational Behavior and Human Decision Processes* 100: 193–201.

Dana, J., R. Weber, and J. Kuang. (2007). "Exploiting Moral Wiggle Room: Experiments Demonstrating an Illusory Preference for Fairness." *Economic Theory* 33: 67–80.

Dancy, Jonathan. (2000). *Practical Reality.* Oxford: Oxford University Press.

Darley, J. and C. Batson. (1973). "'From Jerusalem to Jericho:' A Study of Situational and Dispositional Variables in Helping Behavior." *Journal of Personality and Social Psychology* 27: 100–108.

Darwall, Stephen. (1983). *Impartial Reason.* Ithaca: Cornell University Press.

Doris, John. (1998). "Persons, Situations, and Virtue Ethics." *Noûs* 32: 504–530.

  (2002). *Lack of Character: Personality and Moral Behavior.* Cambridge: Cambridge University Press.

  (2010). "Heated Agreement: *Lack of Character* as *Being for the Good*." *Philosophical Studies* 148: 135–146.

Dreier, James. (1990). "Internalism and Speaker Relativism." *Ethics* 101: 6–26.

Driver, Julia. (2001). *Uneasy Virtue.* Cambridge: Cambridge University Press.

Feinberg, Joel. (1958). "Psychological Egoism," Reprinted in *Reason and Responsibility.* Ed. Joel Feinberg and Russ Shafer-Landau. Sixteenth Edition (2017). Boston: Centage Learning, 561–573.

Forsythe, R., J. Horowitz, N. Savin, and M. Sefton. (1994). "Fairness in Simple Bargaining Experiments." *Games and Economic Behavior* 6: 347–369.

Frankfurt, Harry. (1988). "Rationality and the Unthinkable," in *The Importance of What We Care About.* Cambridge: Cambridge University Press, 177–190.

  (1993). "On the Necessity of Ideals," in *Moral Self.* Ed. G. Noam and T. Wren. Cambridge: MIT Press, 16–27. Reprinted in *Volition, Necessity, and Love.* Cambridge: Cambridge University Press, 108–116.

  (2002). "Reply to Gary Watson," in *Contours of Agency: Essays on Themes from Harry Frankfurt.* Ed. Sarah Buss and Lee Overton. Cambridge: MIT Press, 160–164.

Greene, J. and J. Haidt. (2002) "How (and Where) Does Moral Judgment Work?" *TRENDS in Cognitive Science* 6: 517–523.

Haidt, J. (2001) "The Emotional Dog and Its Rational Tail: A Social Intuitionist Approach to Moral Judgment." *Psychological Review* 108: 814–834.

  (2003) "The Emotional Dog Does Learn New Tricks: A Reply to Pizarro and Bloom (2003)." *Psychological Review* 110: 197–198.

Haidt, J. and F. Bjorklund. (2008a) "Social Intuitionists Answer Six Questions about Moral Psychology," in *Moral Psychology. The Cognitive Science of Morality: Intuition and Diversity.* Ed. Walter Sinnott-Armstrong. Volume 2. Cambridge: MIT Press, 181–217.

(2008b) "Social Intuitionists Reason, in Conversation," in *Moral Psychology. The Cognitive Science of Morality: Intuition and Diversity.* Ed. Walter Sinnott-Armstrong. Volume 2. Cambridge: MIT Press, 241–254.

Haidt, J. and C. Joseph. (2004) "Intuitive Ethics: How Innately Prepared Intuitions Generate Culturally Variable Virtues." *Daedalus* 133: 55–66.

Haney, C., C. Banks, and P. Zimbardo. (1973). "A Study of Prisoners and Guards in a Simulated Prison," in *Readings about the Social Animal.* Ed. E. Aronson. Third Edition. San Francisco: Freeman, 52–67.

Harman, Gilbert. (1999). "Moral Philosophy meets Social Psychology: Virtue Ethics and the Fundamental Attribution Error." *Proceedings of the Aristotelian Society* 99: 315–331.

(2000). "The Nonexistence of Character Traits." *Proceedings of the Aristotelian Society* 100: 223–226.

(2001). "Virtue Ethics without Character Traits," in *Fact and Value.* Ed. A. Byrne, R. Stalnaker, and R. Wedgewood. Cambridge: MIT Press, 117–127.

(2003). "No Character or Personality." *Business Ethics Quarterly* 13: 87–94.

(2009). "Skepticism about Character Traits." *The Journal of Ethics* 13: 235–242.

Horgan, Terry and Mark Timmons. (2007). "Morphological Rationalism and the Psychology of Moral Judgment." *Ethical Theory and Moral Practice* 10: 279–295.

(forthcoming). *Illuminating Reasons: An Essay in Moral Phenomenology.*

Hursthouse, Rosalind. (1981). "A False Doctrine of the Mean." *Proceedings of the Aristotelian Society* 81: 57–72.

Isen, A. and P. Levin. (1972). "Effect of Feeling Good on Helping: Cookies and Kindness." *Journal of Personality and Social Psychology* 21: 384–388.

Jacobson, Daniel. (2008). "Does Social Intuitionism Flatter Morality or Challenge It?" in *Moral Psychology. The Cognitive Science of Morality: Intuition and Diversity.* Ed. Walter Sinnott-Armstrong. Volume 2. Cambridge: MIT Press, 219–232.

Kahneman, D., J. Knetsch, and R. Thaler. (1986). "Fairness and the Assumptions of Economics." *Journal of Business* 59: S285–S300.

Kohlberg, L. (1969) "Stage and Sequence: The Cognitive-Developmental Approach to Socialization," in *Handbook of Socialization Theory and Research.* Ed. David Goslin. Chicago: Rand McNally and Company, 347–480.

Kristjánsson, Kristján. (2008). "An Aristotelian Critique of Situationism." *Philosophy* 83: 55–76.

Latané, B. and J. Darley. (1970). *The Unresponsive Bystander: Why Doesn't He Help?* New York: Appleton-Century-Crofts.

Latané, B. and J. Rodin. (1969). "A Lady in Distress: Inhibiting Effects of Friends and Strangers on Bystander Intervention." *Journal of Experimental Social Psychology* 5: 189–202.

List, J. (2007). "On the Interpretation of Giving in Dictator Games." *Journal of Political Economy* 115: 482–493.

May, Joshua. (2018). *Regard for Reason in the Moral Mind.* Oxford: Oxford University Press.

McDowell, John. (1978). "Are Moral Requirements Hypothetical Imperatives?" *Proceedings of the Aristotelian Society Supplement* 52: 13–42.

McPherson, Tristram. (2020). *Epistemology and Methodology in Ethics.* Cambridge: Cambridge University Press.

Mele, Alfred. (2003). *Motivation and Agency.* New York: Oxford University Press.

Merritt, Maria, John Doris, and Gilbert Harman. (2010). "Character," in *The Moral Psychology Handbook.* Ed. J. Doris and the Moral Psychology Research Group. Oxford: Oxford University Press, 355–401.

Mikhail, J. (2011). *Elements of Moral Cognition.* Cambridge: Cambridge University Press.

Milgram, S. (1974). *Obedience to Authority.* New York: Harper & Row.

Miller, Christian. (2008a). "Motivational Internalism." *Philosophical Studies* 139: 233–255.

(2008b). "Motivation in Agents." *Noûs* 42: 222–266.

(2011). "Overview of Contemporary Metaethics and Normative Theory," in *The Continuum Companion to Ethics.* Ed. Christian Miller. London: Continuum Press, xiv–lii.

(2013). *Moral Character: An Empirical Theory.* Oxford: Oxford University Press.

(2014). *Character and Moral Psychology.* Oxford: Oxford University Press.

(2015). "Distributive Justice and Empirical Moral Psychology." *Stanford Encyclopedia of Philosophy.* http://plato.stanford.edu/entries/justice-moral-psych/.

(2016). "Assessing Two Competing Approaches to the Psychology of Moral Judgments," *Philosophical Explorations* 19: 28–47.

(2017). "Categorizing Character: Moving Beyond the Aristotelian Framework," in *Varieties of Virtue Ethics.* Ed. David Carr. London: Palgrave Macmillan, 143–162.

(2019a). "Some Philosophical Concerns about How the VIA Classifies Character Traits and the VIA-IS Measures Them." *Journal of Positive Psychology* 14: 6–19.

(2019b). "Rationalism and Intuitionism," in *The Routledge Handbook on Moral Epistemology*. Ed. Mark Timmons, Karen Jones, and Aaron Zimmerman. New York: Routledge, 329–346.

(2020). "Moral Relativism and Virtue," in *Virtues in Theory and Practice: Local or Universal?* Ed. Catherine A. Darnell and Kristján Kristjánsson. Routledge, 11–25.

(2021). *Honesty: The Philosophy and Psychology of a Neglected Virtue.* New York: Oxford University Press.

Narvaez, D. (2008). "The Social Intuitionist Model: Some Counter-Intuitions," in *Moral Psychology. The Cognitive Science of Morality: Intuition and Diversity.* Ed. Walter Sinnott-Armstrong. Volume 2. Cambridge: MIT Press, 233–240.

Nichols, Shaun. (2004). *Sentimental Rules: On the Natural Foundations of Moral Judgment.* Oxford: Oxford University Press.

Nussbaum, M. (1988). "Non-Relative Virtues: An Aristotelian Approach." *Midwest Studies in Philosophy* 13: 32–53.

Peterson, C. and M. Seligman (Eds.). 2004. *Character Strengths and Virtues: A Handbook and Classification.* Oxford: Oxford University Press.

Pizarro, D. and P. Bloom. (2003) "The Intelligence of the Moral Intuitions: Comment on Haidt (2001)," *Psychological Review* 110: 193–196.

Plato. (1968). *The Republic of Plato.* Trans. Allan Bloom. New York: Basic Books.

Prinz, Jesse. (2007). *The Emotional Construction of Morals.* Oxford: Oxford University Press.

Rachels, James. (1986). *The Elements of Moral Philosophy.* New York: Random House.

Railton, Peter. (2014) "The Affective Dog and Its Rational Tale: Intuition and Attunement," *Ethics* 124: 813–859.

Rosati, Connie. (2016). "Moral Motivation." *Stanford Encyclopedia of Philosophy.* https://plato.stanford.edu/entries/moral-motivation/.

Roskies, Adina. (2003). "Are Ethical Judgments Intrinsically Motivational? Lessons from 'Acquired Sociopathy'." *Philosophical Psychology* 16: 51–66.

Sauer, Hanno. (2011) "Social Intuitionism and the Psychology of Moral Reasoning," *Philosophy Compass* 6: 708–721.

Scanlon, T. M. (1998). *What We Owe to Each Other.* Cambridge: Belknap Press of Harvard University Press.

Shafer-Landau, Russ. (2003a). *Whatever Happened to Good and Evil?* Oxford: Oxford University Press.

(2003b). *Moral Realism: A Defence.* Oxford: Clarendon Press.

Smith, Michael. (1987). "The Humean Theory of Motivation." *Mind* 96: 36–61.

(1994). *The Moral Problem*. Oxford: Blackwell Publishers.

Sneddon, Andrew. (2007) "A Social Model of Moral Dumbfounding: Implications for Studying Moral Reasoning and Moral Judgment," *Philosophical Psychology* 20: 731–748.

Sobel, David and David Copp. (2001). "Against Direction of Fit Accounts of Belief and Desire." *Analysis* 61: 44–53.

Solomon, Robert. (2003). "Victims of Circumstances? A Defense of Virtue Ethics in Business." *Business Ethics Quarterly* 13: 43–62.

Stich, Stephen, John Doris, and Erica Roedder. (2010). "The Science of Altruism," in *The Moral Psychology Handbook*. Eds. J. Doris and the Moral Psychology Research Group. Oxford: Oxford University Press, 147–205.

Stocker, Michael. (1976). "The Schizophrenia of Modern Ethical Theories." *The Journal of Philosophy* 73: 453–466.

(1979). "Desiring the Bad: An Essay in Moral Psychology." *The Journal of Philosophy* 76: 738–753.

Svavarsdóttir, Sigrún. (1999). "Moral Cognitivism and Motivation." *The Philosophical Review* 108: 161–219.

Tiberius, Valerie. (2015). *Moral Psychology: A Contemporary Introduction*. New York: Routledge.

Timmons, Mark. (2012). *Moral Theory: An Introduction*. Lanham: Rowman and Littlefield.

Toi, M. and C. Batson. (1982). "More Evidence that Empathy is a Source of Altruistic Motivation." *Journal of Personality and Social Psychology* 43: 281–292.

Turri, John. (2009). "The Ontology of Epistemic Reasons." *Noûs* 43: 490–512.

Van Roojen, Mark. (2018). "Moral Cognitivism versus Non-Cognitivism." *Stanford Encyclopedia of Philosophy*. https://stanford.library.sydney.edu.au /entries/moral-cognitivism/index.html.

Acknowledgments

I am very grateful to Dale Miller and Ben Eggleston for inviting me to contribute to the Elements series, and for being extremely patient with delays on my end. Thanks also to Dale Miller, Ben Eggleston, and two reviewers for Cambridge for their very helpful comments on the manuscript. Finally, my heartfelt thanks to Joyous Miller for her detailed feedback and for always pushing me to write more accessibly and clearly.

For permission to use portions of my previous work, I am grateful to several publishers. All specific references and acknowledgments of permission to use previous work are found in footnotes in the text.

Finally, as always, I am deeply appreciative of all the support from my wife, Jessie Lee Miller, my children Jackson, William, and Lillian, my parents Bill and Joyous Miller, and my mother-in-law Eileen Smith.

About the Author

Christian B. Miller is the A. C. Reid Professor of Philosophy at Wake Forest University. He is the author of over 90 academic papers as well as four books with Oxford University Press, *Moral Character: An Empirical Theory* (2013), *Character and Moral Psychology* (2014), *The Character Gap: How Good Are We?* (2017), and *Honesty: The Philosophy and Psychology of a Neglected Virtue* (2021). He has also edited or co-edited five additional books. Miller is a science contributor for *Forbes*, and his writings have also appeared in *The New York Times, Wall Street Journal, Dallas Morning News, Slate, The Conversation, Newsweek, Aeon,* and *Christianity Today.*

To Michael DePaul

My extraordinary dissertation supervisor and a far better philosopher than I will ever be.

Cambridge Elements

Ethics

Ben Eggleston
University of Kansas
Ben Eggleston is a professor of philosophy at the University of Kansas. He is the editor of John Stuart Mill, *Utilitarianism: With Related Remarks from Mill's Other Writings* (Hackett, 2017) and a co-editor of *Moral Theory and Climate Change: Ethical Perspectives on a Warming Planet* (Routledge, 2020), *The Cambridge Companion to Utilitarianism* (Cambridge, 2014), and *John Stuart Mill and the Art of Life* (Oxford, 2011). He is also the author of numerous articles and book chapters on various topics in ethics.

Dale E. Miller
Old Dominion University, Virginia
Dale E. Miller is a professor of philosophy at Old Dominion University. He is the author of *John Stuart Mill: Moral, Social and Political Thought* (Polity, 2010) and a co-editor of *Moral Theory and Climate Change: Ethical Perspectives on a Warming Planet* (Routledge, 2020), *A Companion to Mill* (Blackwell, 2017), *The Cambridge Companion to Utilitarianism* (Cambridge, 2014), *John Stuart Mill and the Art of Life* (Oxford, 2011), and *Morality, Rules, and Consequences: A Critical Reader* (Edinburgh, 2000). He is also the editor-in-chief of *Utilitas*, and the author of numerous articles and book chapters on various topics in ethics broadly construed.

About the Series
This Elements series provides an extensive overview of major figures, theories, and concepts in the field of ethics. Each entry in the series acquaints students with the main aspects of its topic while articulating the author's distinctive viewpoint in a manner that will interest researchers.

Cambridge Elements ≡

Ethics

Elements in the Series

Printed in the United States
by Baker & Taylor Publisher Services